THE
GLOBAL VEGET

MRIDU SHAILAJ-THANKI
JUHEE PRABHA RATHOR
VANDANA SHAILAJ-THANKI

Illustrations
SUHITA MITRA

B&S
Body & Soul Books

ISBN 978-93-81576-45-8
© Text: Mridu Shailaj Thanki, Juhee Prabha Rathor, Vandana Shailaj-Thanki, 2014
© Illustrations: Leadstart Publishing Pvt Ltd
Cover, Illustrations & Artworks Suhita Mitra
Printing   Lifon Industries

Published in India, 2014
BODY & SOUL BOOKS
An imprint of
LEADSTART PUBLISHING PVT LTD
Trade Centre, Level 1, Bandra Kurla Complex, Bandra (E), Mumbai 400 051, INDIA
T + 91 22 40700804   F +91 22 40700800 **E** info@leadstartcorp.com **W** www.leadstartcorp.com
US Office Axis Corp, 7845 E Oakbrook Circle, Madison, WI 53717, USA

All rights reserved worldwide
No part of this publication may be reproduced, stored in or introduced into a retrieval system, or transmitted, in any form, or by any means (electronic, mechanical, photocopying, recording or otherwise), without the prior permission of the Publisher. Any person who commits an unauthorized act in relation to this publication can be liable to criminal prosecution and civil claims for damages.

*To our families ~
who have inspired valuable recipe ideas and have always been there
not only to taste and comment on our creations but also to
provide constructive advice, TLC and support at crucial times.
And to Ila Goel Rallan, our niece in Mumbai ~
without whose help this book would not have been possible.*

ABOUT THE AUTHORS

Mridu Shailaj Thanki was born in India and lives in the UK, raising her two children and working in the public and voluntary sectors at a senior level. Her passion for cookery goes back to her childhood. Mridu's extensive travels exposed her to diverse cultures and cuisines while honing her culinary skills. She has run cookery classes in different parts of the world and has appeared on British Television. In 2009, she published her first book on vegetarian food, *Feasts of India*. She has also co-authored a book on children living in poverty, *Our Lives and Hopes; Beyond Statistics and Reports* (2006).

Juhee Prabha Rathor was born in Kenya and lives in London. A practising lawyer, with a background in psychotherapy, training and coaching, she has an abiding interest in gastronomy and nutrient-rich foods for optimal performance. Juhee is fascinated by cross-cultural cuisines and the role of food in connecting communities and regions around the world. She experiments extensively with global recipes and enjoys creating her own range of healthy, enjoyable and innovative dishes. Juhee blogs about all things foodie and healthy at http://foodwiz4u.blogspot.co.uk .

Vandana Shailaj-Thanki was born in India and grew up in Mumbai, one of the most cosmopolitan cities in the country. Although a vegetarian she further developed a palate for and interest in diverse vegetarian cuisines. A social worker by profession, Vandana has worked in children's social care, including children with disabilities. She moved to the UK many years ago. Living in London provided her with opportunities to develop her love of cooking and experimenting with both new and tried and tested recipes from all over the world. Vandana especially enjoys baking and making desserts. She recently took up weaving using a table loom, translating her keen interest in the arts and crafts into practice.

ABOUT THE ILLUSTRATOR

Suhita Mitra was born in Kohima, Nagaland – a region of untouched, natural beauty. Such an environment was a natural nursery for the imagination. Suhita joined the National Institute Of Design, Ahmedabad, where the untrammelled imagination fostered by her childhood environment, found meaningful channels through art appreciation, photography, freehand drawing, animation and typography. She continues to find inspiration in nature for her work as an illustrator and designer.

~ CONTENTS ~

Introduction 10
Vegetarianism 13
Techniques 15

All recipes serve 4-5 people unless otherwise indicated

BREAKFAST & BRUNCH

Almond Croissants *France* 21
Avocado Bruschetta *Italy* 22
English Breakfast *UK* 23
Crêpes with Savoury Filling *France* 24
Oatmeal Porridge *UK* 26
Quesadilla *Mexico* 27
Rösti *Switzerland/Germany* 29
Scrambled Eggs with Fenugreek *Kenya* 30
Shakshuka *Mediterranean* 31
Toast with Spinach *USA* 32
Vegetarian Frittata *Italy* 33

SNACKS & TID-BITS

Cheese on Toast *Europe* 35
Chocolate-Marzipan Tart *Europe* 36
Date & Nut Roll *Europe* 37
Griddle Cakes *UK* 38
Latke *Germany/Israel* 39
Mogo with Coconut Milk *Kenya* 40
Oat Scones *UK* 41
Savoury Muffins *Europe* 42
Spinach Drops *UK* 43
Welsh Rarebit *UK* 44

LUNCH & DINNER

Soups

Bori-Bori Soup *Paraguay* 47
Broccoli & Blue Cheese Soup *Europe* 48
Chickpea & Vegetable Catalan Soup *Spain* 49
Garlic & Paprika Soup *Spain* 50
Gazpacho *Spain* 51
Leek with Potatoes *Germany* 52
Onion Soup *France* 53
Peasant Soup *Italy* 55
Sopa de Ajo Blanco *Spain* 56
Soup au Pistou *France* 57

Starters

From Greece, Turkey, Middle East, the Mediterranean & Spain

Aubergine with Nuts 60
Babaganoush 61
Broad Beans Salad 62
Charred Capsicum 63
Chickpeas with Spinach Tapa 64
Dolmas 65
Hummus 67
Marinated Olives 68
Oven-Dried Tomatoes 69
Patatas Bravas 70
Potato Salad 71

Mains

Aubergine Parmigiana *Italy* 74	Onion Flan *UK* 101
Bread Gnocchi *UK/Italy* 75	Pasta with Aubergine *Italy* 103
Bulgur Wheat with Sunflower Seeds *Greece, Turkey, Middle East* 76	Penne with Mozzarella *Italy* 104
	Red Curry *Thailand* 105
Butter Beans in Pizzaiola Sauce *Italy* 77	Ribbon Pasta with Roast Peppers & Olives *Italy* 107
Cannelloni *Italy* 78	
Chickpeas & Aubergine *Lebanon* 80	Roasted Vegetable Slice *Mediterranean* 108
Chickpeas with Mogo *E. Africa* 81	
Chilli con Queso *Mexico* 82	Shepherd's Pie *UK* 109
Corn-on-Cob Sabzi *Kenya* 83	Sopa Paraguay *Paraguay* 110
Dairy Heaven *UK/USA* 84	Spinach with Coconut Milk & Peanuts *East Africa* 111
Feijoada Bean Stew *Brazil* 85	
Green Curry *Thailand* 87	Spinach Quiche *France* 112
Haggis *Scotland* 89	Stuffed Zucchini *Europe* 114
Kafta Bil Tahini *Lebanon* 91	Tofu, Vegetables & Cashew Stir-fry *China* 115
Kidney Beans & Spinach *Kenya* 93	
Lablabi *Tunisia* 94	Vegetables Roast *Greece* 116
Lasagne with Aubergine *Argentina* .. 95	Vegetarian Cacciatore *Italy* 117
Maharagwe ya Nazi *Kenya* 96	Vegetarian Salade Nicoise *France* 119
Meal-in-a-Bowl *Sudan* 98	
Mushroom & Parsley Open Lasagne *Italy* 100	

Sides

Apple Sauce *Germany* 122	Broccoli with Orange & Almonds *Europe* 125
Aubergine with Mozzarella *Italy* 123	
Broccoli with Nuts *Europe* 124	Cauliflower with Potatoes *Greece* 126

Corn in Buttermilk *Kenya* 127
Corn Khichdi *Kenya* 128
Guacamole *Mexico* 129
Mushrooms in Cream *Azerbaijan* 130
Okra *Middle East* 131
Pineapple Relish *India* 132
Potato Mash *UK* 133
Potato Skins *Mexico* 134
Potatoes with Sesame Seeds & Olives
Mediterranean 135
Pumpkin with Yoghurt *Afghanistan*... 136
Roast Potatoes *UK* 137
Roast Pumpkin with Seeds *Europe* 138
Sliced Potatoes with Cream *Latvia* 139
Spicy Aubergine *Portugal* 140
Spinach with Yoghurt *Iran* 141
Stuffed Capsicum *Europe* 141
Vegetarian Medley *Mediterranean* 143

Salads

Apple & Celery Salad *USA* 145
Avocado & Orange Salad
Mediterranean 146
Beetroot Salad with Dill *Europe* 147
Carrot with Lemon *Cuba* 148
Carrot with Peanuts *Mediterranean* 148
Classic Greek Salad *Greece* 149
Zucchini Dip *Mediterranean* 150
Crunchy Salad *Europe* 151
De Puy Lentil Warm Salad *France* 152
Fennel & Tomato Salad *Europe* 153
Fennel, Carrot & Orange Salad
Mediterranean 154
Green Bean Salad *Europe* 155
Green Lentil Salad *Greece* 156
Green Potato Salad
Iran/Morocco/Turkey 157
Panzanella *Italy* 158
Potatoes with Sour Cream & Herbs
Europe 159
Quinoa Herby Salad *Middle East* 160
Red Cabbage with Nuts *Ukraine* 161
Red Melon & Feta Salad
Mediterranean 162
Shredded Salad with Tahini Dressing
Middle East 163
Sprouted Bean Salad *Europe* 164
Tomatoes with Pine Nuts
Mediterranean 165
Tomato Salsa *Mexico* 166
Vietnamese Salad *Vietnam* 167
Zucchini Salad *Europe* 168

Dressings

Vinaigrette *France* 169
Harissa Paste
Mediterranean/N. Africa 170
Honey Vinaigrette *France* 171
Lemon Mayonnaise *Europe* 171

Desserts & Afters

Apple Crumble *UK* 173
Apple & Plum Cake *Europe* 174
Cake Pudding with Orange *Brazil* 175
Dry Fruits & Nuts Compote,
Middle East 176
Greek Style Semolina Cake *Greece* 177
Irish Coffee Cake *Europe* 178
Panjeeri *India* 179
Pears with Saffron & Honey
Middle East 180
Pineapple Upside Down Cake
UK 181
Summer Pudding *UK* 182
Trifle *UK* 183

Select Glossary 185
Alphabetical Index of Dishes 187

INTRODUCTION

Is it not delightful to have friends [food] coming from distant quarters? ~ Confucius

Enjoying a vegetarian meal locally or while globe-trotting, is far less challenging and much more pleasurable than it used to be even a few years ago. Also, there is now easier access to a wide range of ingredients if one wishes to cook meals from different cuisines, at home. As the approaches to different cuisines vary, sometimes in significant ways, we suggest that you read through the *Techniques* section of the book first in order to gain a better understanding of both the recipes and the methods used.

We, the co-authors, have been good friends for years. While we have our individual personalities and ways of life, we also have many common likes and dislikes. The one interest we passionately share, our love of food – cooking, feeding and eating – has been central to our lives. This global collection of recipes represents our collective enthusiasm for sharing with everyone all things related to the culinary arts. All of us have travelled extensively around the globe and spent long periods in various countries. This has given us the opportunity to enjoy a variety of cuisines. Also, our home base in London, presents us with easy access to a mind-boggling choice of food from all over the world. We have been richly blessed to have been able to indulge our passion for food to the hilt. Not only have we sampled many cuisines, we have also collated the recipes which we believe will appeal to vegetarians and non-vegetarians alike.

Although our travels have not been specifically gastronomic in intent, what fascinated us everywhere was the ability of humans to prepare food creatively. Using the same ingredients, individuals produce such different tastes. We have observed how an ingredient can be cooked in such diverse ways, with slight variations – to create unique dishes with tantalising colours, flavours and aromas.

This book provides neither an extensive nor an exhaustive list of vegetarian recipes. It is simply a selection of dishes we consider an appropriate reflection of various places and people, and the food they relish, as we too have come to do.

The recipes can be placed in three categories.

1. **Travelogue recipes**: collected from family and friends in different parts of the world, these recipes represent mainly the staple food of the country. Travelling around the world one can find an endless assortment of tasty, healthy vegetarian food – even in the places with the most carnivorous cuisines, people do create delightful fare for discerning vegetarians. Needless to say, often one can find similarities of dishes within a region e.g. the Mediterranean and the Middle East. And yet there are some clearly unique preparations. These recipes are not elaborate or fancy dishes of a gourmet variety. They embody food that people of these far flung places would eat at home mostly daily – dishes prepared from ingredients sourced within the country. The recipes therefore are plain, down to earth and not too technical. We feel that it is home-cooking that gives one the true flavour of a country or a place.

2. **Recipes from our doorstep**: in London, world food is so easily available – grocers and restaurants from Zanzibar to Azerbaijan covering all possible global fare – and is a constant temptation for foodies like us. It's like being in food heaven. The recipes in this category are based on us working out the ingredients and method of cooking through trial and error. Often it has taken 4-5 tryouts before achieving the desired result. For example, we tasted for the very first time Pumpkin with Yoghurt, in an Afghan restaurant. While all the dishes we tried were great, somehow the subtle flavours and taste of this one stayed with us. All the five senses worked together and we managed to reproduce it to perfection after three attempts.

3. **Recipes of creative imagination**: often we have come across food or recipes that are enticing but as some of the ingredients are not suitable for us vegetarians we have put our mind to it and adapted them to suit us. Mexican Chilli, is one such example. It didn't take us long to substitute crumbled *paneer* for mincemeat, its basic ingredient. Some of the dishes are our own inventions created simply to broaden our repertoire of vegetarian choices. Spinach Drops is one such dish.

The book has been presented so that you become familiar with the processes and components involved in cooking certain meals before you get to the recipes. The section on *Vegetarianism* briefly shares the history and practice of vegetarianism globally; while the *Techniques* section, provides suggestions on how to achieve the best results. The *recipes* start with *Breakfast & Brunch* and end with *Desserts & Afters*. They cover all possible meal and snack times.

Cooking is an art. Although it is hard work, it is worthwhile and rewarding for both the cook and the diner. This book helps you to bring the world to your table. We hope you will share our passion and try out these recipes with your family and friends.

VEGETARIANISM

Preserve the old, but know the new. ~ Chinese Proverb

The origins of vegetarianism can be traced back to ancient India. Pythagoras, the Greek mathematician, scientist and philosopher, promoted it in the West. Vegetarianism is broadly understood to mean the practice of following a plant-based diet and the exclusion of all meats, including sea creatures and animal by-products. The belief in the sanctity of all life and the principle of *ahimsa* (non-violence), by the Hindus, Buddhists and Jains, expanded the practice of vegetarianism in Asia, long before the Christian era. While Judaism, Christianity and Islam all have strong connections to the Biblical ideal of the Garden of Eden and a herbivorous diet, only minorities within these religious groups actually practice and advocate such diets.

Although vegetarianism has been practiced for many centuries, the term *vegetarian* was coined by the British Vegetarian Society in the mid-1800s. Being a vegetarian has ultimately been a matter of individual, voluntary choice. Vegetarians are a diverse group differentiated not only by their personal backgrounds and values but also by what motivates them to remain vegetarian or 'convert' to a vegetarian diet. Motivating factors for remaining or becoming a vegetarian include religious, ethical, practical, health and economic considerations.

The treatment of animals and awareness about the food we eat and its impact on our health, has gained significant attention in recent years. The adverse effect of red meat, the unethical methods of farming, (to name just a couple of issues), have influenced many people to alter their eating habits. Research too, has progressively shown a vegetarian diet to be healthier. The *5 a day* health initiative in the UK, based on these findings, emphasises the importance of having five portions of fruits and vegetables daily.

Apart from being the country where vegetarianism originated, India has the single largest population of vegetarians (around 40%), in the world. This is reflected in India's diverse and extensive vegetarian cuisines that have tantalised and inspired food lovers the world over. Not so long ago, it was quite a challenge for vegetarians travelling to different parts of the world (for example, mainland Europe), to find a balanced meal and/or something healthy and tasty to eat. With the growth in international travel and greater awareness regarding food and its related issues, the number of vegetarians in the world has grown significantly. Cultural exchanges and crossovers have helped to promote vegetarianism, particularly in Europe and the USA. The stereotypical image of a vegetarian – long-haired, wearing sandals and eating lentil soup and sprouts – is now firmly in the past. Most major European cities now have vegetarian restaurants or eateries with a reasonable choice of vegetarian dishes on their menu. However, they often offer *nouvelle cuisine* or food at the expensive end of the spectrum. In Britain, vegetarianism is gaining ever more support. Besides the growth of exclusively vegetarian outlets, vegetarian food/meals are also available in most restaurants and cafés throughout the country. In fact, Britain established the first Vegetarian Society in 1847, and surprisingly, almost 10% of the country's population currently practices vegetarianism.

Although in some quarters vegetarianism is still seen as 'special' or 'different', there are now Vegetarian Societies in almost every country in the world, covering the five continents. They promote the concept of vegetarianism, offer information on the benefits of such a diet, and often list vegetarian outlets in that country. With increasing access to ingredients that enable wider cooking options at home and a broad choice outside, one can look forward to the day when vegetarianism will become integral to the mainstream culinary experience. We hope *The Global Vegetarian* will go some way towards contributing to that.

TECHNIQUES

Cooking food from an unfamiliar cuisine can often appear daunting because of the newness of the ingredients and methods. However, a love of cooking and a basic understanding of the ingredients and techniques (plus some daring-do), not only helps to produce tasty, wholesome dishes but goes a long way towards making the experience of food preparation simpler, smoother, less time consuming, and ultimately more rewarding.

Before starting on a recipe, ensure you have all the ingredients or a close substitute if necessary, and work out clearly the sequence. Both physical and mental preparation is crucial when launching into unfamiliar territory. Some of the methods described in this book have been derived directly from local cooks. Other techniques are not traditional and have been developed through experimentation. The recipes **serve four to five people**. In general, however, it is better to prepare meals in quantities that allow people to have more than one helping. We also list a few ideas/hints which we consider cooks will find constructive.

EXPLANATIONS

Adding salt and pepper: it is best to season food by adding/adjusting these vital ingredients to taste.

Al dente: the term comes from Italian, meaning 'to the tooth/bite'. Pasta should be cooked so that it is firm but not hard and has some resistance in the centre when chewed. *Al dente* pasta has a lower glycaemic index. Follow the cooking instructions on the pasta packet and after boiling for 6-7 minutes, test the pasta. If it needs more time, keep boiling but taste every 1-2 minutes till the desired firmness has been achieved. Rice, beans or vegetables can be cooked *al dente* if it enhances the taste of a dish.

Blanching: meaning 'to whiten' is a form of parboiling. See below.
To blanch fruits/vegetables, bring a large pot of water to the boil, adding enough salt so the water tastes like sea water. Have another bowl big enough for the amount of food, ready with ice water. Add the fruits/vegetables to the boiling water. Cook for the prescribed time, then drain and transfer to the ice water. Drain once cool and pat dry.

Blanching helps to loosen the skin, making it easier to peel (e.g. tomatoes, peaches). It can also give a crisp but tender texture to the food.

Blind baking: blind baking a pie crust before filling it, is crucial to prevent the bottom of your quiche, flan or tart, from turning soggy. To blind bake, spread the pastry in the pastry tin/dish. Prick with a fork so that air is released and the pastry does not rise in the centre. Cover with parchment paper/ aluminium foil. Finally fill with **baking beans**/ uncooked beans/rice. Bake as directed in the recipe.

Parboil: parboiling or leaching or blanching, is to partially cook food by boiling before roasting, stir-frying, baking, sautéing or removing the skin from fruits and vegetables. Add the ingredients to boiling water and cook until slightly soft. The time taken to parboil depends on the food item and recipe.

Roasting: in this method, food is cooked using dry heat in an oven or on an open flame. Generally, vegetables can lose some of their vitamins and minerals through the cooking process but roasting helps to retain the nutritional value and flavour of food.

Sauté: from the French *sautér* (to jump), it refers to the tossing of food as it is cooked. Sautéing cooks food quickly by browning it and retaining its texture and flavour. This method of cooking works best if the food is cut into small bite-sized pieces/thin slices or if the food is already tender.

TIPS & SUGGESTIONS FOR FOOD PEPARATION/TIME & ENERGY SAVING

Learnt through experience and/or picked up from family/friends, the following tips and suggestions will help make things simpler and add to the joy in cooking and feeding your family and friends.

- Soak beans overnight and lentils for 3-4 hours before cooking to save time and energy.
- Soak rice for 10-15 minutes before cooking for the same reason – saving time and energy. Also rice cooks better.
- Ingredients such as onion, garlic or ginger, can be prepared well in advance for a party meal. They can be chopped as required a few days before and stored in airtight tubs in the fridge.
- Onions can be fried in advance in oil/butter/as suggested in a recipe, and stored in an airtight tub for 2-3 days in the fridge. This will save time when you are cooking several dishes, even if it is not for a large number of people.
- For day-to-day cooking, you can keep peeled cloves of garlic sealed in a bag in the fridge for 7-10 days. Or you can chop the garlic or make a paste and then store and use as required.
- When boiling potatoes, boil a few extra and store them when cool, in the fridge for up to 3-4 days. These can then be used at any time to make a quick snack or meal.
- Most leftovers, except rice and potatoes, can be frozen for future use or be given a new incarnation.
- When cooking several dishes for a party, for example, cook the dishes one after the other, using one good pot. As the first item is being cooked get the next one ready for cooking. As soon as the first item is done, transfer it to an oven/microwave-proof serving dish. Use the same pot, after a quick rinse, to start cooking the next dish. This will save water for washing utensils as well as time. It will also enable you to efficiently serve the dishes at the table when required.
- Salads and dressings can be prepared in advance; add the dressing just before serving.
- When baking, maximise the use of the oven and save energy at the same time, by baking more than one item if possible.
- Cooking in a mix of olive oil and butter prevents the butter from burning. It also brings

in the health benefits of olive oil and the flavour of butter, to the dish.
- Avoid repeating ingredients in the same meal (e.g. pasta with tomato sauce and tomato salad).
- To make crisp wilting or limp lettuce, empty 1-2 trays of ice cubes in a large bowl and place the lettuce leaves in the bowl. Pour sufficient cold water to cover them. Soak for half an hour. Dry in a salad spinner or with paper towels.
- Similarly, you can make crisp grated or chopped carrots by placing them in ice water and soaking for an hour or so.
- To stop salad from going soggy or watery, you can prepare the salad in advance but add the salt (if using) or salad dressing shortly before serving.
- As with all meals, a vegetarian meal must be nutritionally balanced, therefore it is important to plan a menu that reflects variety.

MEASUREMENTS USED
Weights: Depending on the type of vegetable/ingredient in some recipes, the required quantity is specified in terms of its weight (kg, gm), size (cm) or number (4, 2-3).
Cup: a cup = 240 ml, as it is a measurement of volume
Conversion into weight will depend on the food item being measured, for example:
1 cup flour = 150 gm
1 cup caster/granulated sugar = 225 gm
1 cup grated cheese = 110 gm
1 cup of any liquid = 240 ml, but will vary in weight
tbsp: tablespoon
tsp: teaspoon

OVEN TEMPERATURES
Oven temperatures are specified in Centigrade (C) only, or as:
Low = 160°C, **Moderate** = 180°C – 190°C and **Hot** = 200 – 230°C, to reflect the fact that some dishes were tried during our travels and the recipes have been fine-tuned at home after trial and error

UTENSILS
To cook the recipes in this book, you will not require any specialist cooking equipment. However, it will help to have the following: wok; good sized frying pan; heavy based saucepans; baking tins/trays; ovenproof dishes.

BREAKFAST & BRUNCH

In today's fast-paced world, many of us tend to neglect the first meal of the day – breakfast. Yet breakfast is considered the most important meal of the day by nutritionists. A wholesome breakfast sets us up for the rest of the day, giving us the energy and vitality required for hours of work (and play). The breakfast recipes here include quick-fix items such as oats, which are not only healthy but also filling, as well as preparations that are more suitable for days-off when one can have a late elaborate brunch – like a Spanish Frittata followed by Almond Croissants.

ALMOND CROISSANTS
~ EUROPE ~

Most Europeans, particularly the French, enjoy rich food. On the Continent, croissants are served for breakfast, along with butter and jam. Fresh buttery croissants with crisp, crunchy tops and soft insides, are treat enough, but with almond filling, they are just heavenly – the perfect mate for coffee, second only to something chocolaty.

INGREDIENTS
4-6 all-butter croissants
8-12 tbsp almond powder
3-4 tsp sugar
¼ cup double cream
4-6 tbsp flaked almonds, toasted

METHOD
1. Warm the cream in a pan and add in the sugar and almond powder. Simmer on low heat till the sugar has dissolved (should be of spreading consistency). Add spoonful/s of milk if necessary.
2. Spilt the croissants from one side with a knife, taking care the halves remained joined at the edges.
3. Spread spoonfuls of the almond paste inside the croissants and close them.
4. Brush a tiny bit of the paste on top and stick on the almond flakes.
5. Warm in a hot oven for a minute or so and serve.

NOTE
➢ A mixture of chocolate and almond powder also makes a delicious filling.

AVOCADO BRUSCHETTA
~ ITALY ~

The word bruchetta *is a derivative of* bruscare, *meaning 'toast' in the Tuscan dialect. Bruschetta usually has a tomato topping. But whatever the name or topping, it is a scrumptious snack for any time or occasion.*

Ingredients
4-6 thick slices of ciabatta/similar bread
2-3 ripe, medium sized avocados
8-10 tbsp olive oil
1 tsp crushed garlic
1-1½ cups mozzarella, sliced
3-4 sprigs fresh basil
¼ tsp salt
Pepper to taste

Method
1. Peel the avocadoes and slice them into long thin pieces.
2. Blend oil and salt with the garlic.
3. Toast the bread slices lightly and brush them with garlic oil.
4. Place equal amounts of avocado on each toast and dribble ½ tsp of oil.
5. Cover avocado with mozzarella.
6. Warm the toasts in a pre-heated oven (maximum heat) for 1-2 minutes.
7. Dribble any leftover garlic oil on the bruschettas and sprinkle with pepper and garnish with whole leaves of basil. Serve warm.

Notes
Other possible toppings *(do not use mozzarella for any of these)*
- Use finely diced tomatoes and then follow the above recipe.
- Use finely diced cucumber, stoned black olives, and feta cheese (diced into bite-sized cubes). Then follow the above recipe.
- Use charred capsicum salad on toasted ciabatta.

ENGLISH BREAKFAST
~ UK ~

A traditional cooked breakfast has more or less become a thing of the past in Britain. At home, it is prepared as an occasional treat. However, Bed & Breakfast places still offer a plate of fry-ups every morning. The traditional version has meat items, but this is the vegetarian version. A rich and satisfying breakfast sets one up for the day.

INGREDIENTS (Serves 1)
1-2 egg/s
1 large tomato, halved
4-6 button mushrooms
1 medium-sized potato, parboiled
1 small onion, chopped into thick rounds
2 slices bread
Olive oil/butter for shallow frying
Salt & crushed pepper to taste
Fresh parsley for garnishing

METHOD
1. Chop the potato into bite-sized pieces. In a pan, sauté the pieces in a little oil till brown. Sprinkle salt and pepper and set aside.
2. Heat some more oil in the same pan. Put in the tomato halves, mushrooms, onion rings and egg/s. Cook over medium heat for a few minutes. Gently turn around each ingredient without disturbing their arrangement. Sprinkle salt and pepper and transfer the arrangement onto a warmed up plate.
3. Warm the potato on high heat and add to the plate.
4. Oil or butter the bread on both sides and put them into another pan to toast on low heat while the eggs & vegetables are cooking.
5. Serve, decorated with parsley, and fried bread on the side. Follow this up with buttered toasts, marmalade and jam. Tea is definitely needed with this breakfast.

NOTE
➢ Egg can be replaced with a chunk of cheese.

CRÊPES WITH SAVOURY FILLING
~ FRANCE ~

In France, crepés are equivalent to street food, and are available at kiosks everywhere. They are a slightly thinner, more delicate version of pancakes. The fillings can be savoury or sweet. They work well for brunch, a light lunch or even an unusual teatime snack (made a little smaller).

INGREDIENTS
For the Crepés
1½ cups plain flour
1 cup milk
½ cup water
1 large egg
4 tbsp olive oil
Salt to taste
Extra oil for shallow frying
For the Filling (*Prepare 6 equal portions*)
1½ cups grated emmental cheese
3 medium -sized tomatoes, thinly sliced
1 small onion, finely sliced
Salt & pepper to taste
Fresh basil

METHOD
Crepés
1. In a good-sized bowl, blend all the crepé ingredients and whisk thoroughly for 5 minutes or so. The batter should be of a runny consistency. Leave the batter in a warm place for ½ hour.
2. Heat a large frying pan well and brush it with a tsp of oil. Evenly pour in a ladle-full (about ¼ cup) of the batter. Very quickly, spread the batter, covering the pan fully by tilting the pan around. Let it cook for 1-2 minutes till slightly brown and then flip over to the other side. Cook for a minute.

3. While still in the pan, spread a portion of the filling on ½ of the crepé. Fold the other and then fold again to form a triangle.
4. Serve hot on its own, or with a salad on the side.

NOTES
Fillings for the crepés can be modified or created as desired.
- A filling of mushrooms with fried onions is rather enjoyable.
- Cooked and drained spinach flavoured with a knob of butter and bit of garlic, is also delicious.
- If you are planning to serve crepés with a sweet filling, then make sure to reduce the salt in the batter to just a pinch and add 1tbsp sugar.

For a sweet filling, try the following options.
- Stewed apples with a spoonful of whipped cream and ice-cream on the side.
- Slices of fresh ripe mangoes with ice-cream on the side.
- Chunky marmalade with a spoonful of whipped cream and ice-cream on the side.
- Chocolate spread with a spoonful of whipped cream and ice-cream on the side.
- Just sugar and lemon juice sprinkled on the crepés.

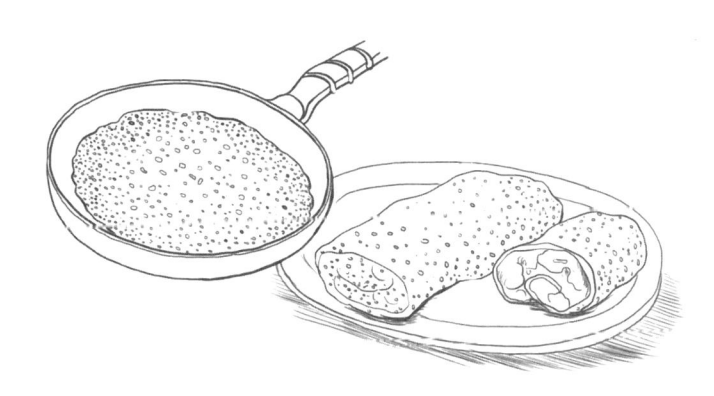

OATMEAL PORRIDGE
~ SCOTLAND ~

Oatmeal is a staple of the Scottish diet but also widely used in other parts of northern Europe. Ground, rolled or 'cut' in different ways and used for making savoury as well as sweet dishes, oatmeal has been extolled for its health benefits. It has been suggested by nutritionists that oatmeal makes for the healthiest breakfast.

INGREDIENTS
2 cups rolled oatmeal
2 cups milk
2 cups water
4 tbsp coarsely ground almonds
½ tsp salt
Sugar to taste (optional)
Extra milk for topping

METHOD
1. **Microwave:** in a large bowl, mix all the ingredients and cook in the microwave for 2 minutes. Open, stir and then cook for another 2 minutes. Serve hot with extra milk on the side.
2. **Cooker:** in a large pot, mix all the ingredients, Cook, stirring constantly over medium heat till it comes to a boil. Lower heat to a minimum and simmer for 4-5 minutes, stirring constantly to prevent it sticking to the bottom of the pot. Serve hot with extra milk.

NOTES
- Chopped dry/fresh fruits can be added to the porridge or served on the side.
- Instead of extra milk, the porridge can be served topped with a spoonful of butter in each bowl.
- Sugar can be replaced with dates or sultanas or a spoonful of jam/marmalade.

QUESADILLA
~ MEXICO ~

Flat bread (tortilla), made with corn flour, is a staple of the Mexican diet. Filled and folded in various ways, tortillas can be turned into tacos, burritos, enchiladas, etc. Wheat tortillas are now common too. Quesadillas are generally made with wheat flour tortillas and can be filled in various ways to make a scrumptious starter or fulsome meal.

INGREDIENTS
For the Tortillas
1¼ cups fine wheat flour
½ cup water
2 tbsp oil
¼ cup flour, for coating the balls
For the Basic Filling
1½-2 cups grated cheese
1 cup finely chopped green onion leaves
A little oil to make the quesadillas

METHOD
Tortillas
1. Mix the flour with the oil and small amounts of water at a time and knead into a springy dough.
2. Leave the dough covered for at least ½ hour. Divide the dough into 6-8 balls.
3. Place a large frying pan on heat (above medium). Coat the balls of dough with dry flour and roll into paper thin rounds of approximately ½ mm thickness.
4. Put the rolled out tortilla into the hot pan. Start rolling the next one while waiting for the first to cook. Give it 20 seconds or so and flip onto the other side. Give it 20 seconds more, then flip back. With a napkin or rolled tissue, gently press the tortilla around the edges. Flip and roast the bottom for 30 seconds and take it off the pan. Follow this process with all the tortillas.

Quesadillas
1. Place the tortilla on a flat surface and spread ¼ cup of cheese on one half.
2. Sprinkle some onion leaves and fold from the middle to make a half-moon shape.
3. Repeat the process with the other tortillas.
4. Place the frying pan on medium heat and spread about a tsp of oil. As soon as the pan heats up, place 2 half-moon quesadillas (making a full moon together), and brown them on both sides. Repeat the process with the rest.
5. Serve the quesadillas hot with various trimmings of your choice.

NOTES
- Different fillings can be added to the basic quesadilla and made into a meal (use your creativity). Some examples:
    1. Cheese + 2 tablespoons of refried beans + chopped green chilli.
    2. Cheese + thin slices of avocado + thin slices of red capsicum + sprinkle of red chilli powder.

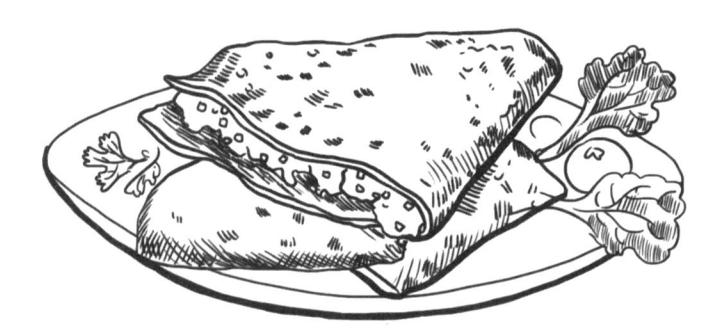

Rösti
~ SWITZERLAND ~

Although rösti has its origin in Germany and was mostly eaten by farmers for breakfast, it is now generally considered a part of Swiss cuisine. Rösti is often served as a side dish to the main meal.

Ingredients
4 large waxy potatoes
6 tbsp butter/olive oil
¼ cup finely chopped fresh parsley
Salt & pepper to taste

Method
1. Wash the potatoes and place them in a good sized pot. Cover with water and parboil for 5 minutes.
Remove from the water and set aside to cool.
2. When cold, skin the potatoes and grate them. Mix in salt and pepper and parsley and divide into two.
3. The rösti should be about 1 cm thick, therefore, choose an appropriately-sized frying pan. Heat 1½ tbsp butter in the pan. As soon as it melts, put in a portion of potato and pat into a round. Let it cook for 3-4 minutes (till it turns brown) and slide onto a serving plate.
4. Heat another 1½ tbsp butter in the pan. As soon as it melts, slide the rösti back in with the uncooked side down. Cook for another 3-4 minutes.
5. Follow the same process with the rest of the potato mixture.
6. Serve hot with sour cream or apple sauce and eggs.

Notes
- ½ cup of grated Gruyere cheese can be added in step 3.
- 1 medium-sized onion (finely chopped), can be added in step 3.
- ½ cup cooked and drained corn kernel can be added in step 3.

SCRAMBLED EGGS WITH FENUGREEK
~ KENYA ~

This dish is quite common in Kenya, where fenugreek (methi) grows abundantly. The bitterness of the fenugreek leaves is mellowed by the creaminess of the scrambled eggs. This is a nourishing and comforting dish.

INGREDIENTS

1 cup fresh fenugreek leaves, washed & finely chopped
4 large eggs, beaten
1 large onion, finely chopped
1 green chilli, finely chopped
2 tbsp butter
1 tbsp vegetable oil
Salt & pepper to taste

METHOD
1. Gently melt the butter in a non-stick saucepan and add in the oil to stop the butter browning.
2. Add the chopped onions and cook over low-medium heat until soft and translucent.
3. Stir in the chilli and sauté for 30 seconds.
4. Add in the fenugreek leaves and cook for about 2 minutes until the leaves have wilted and all the water has evaporated.
5. Keeping the heat low, slowly add in the beaten eggs whilst stirring gently and constantly. The eggs should cook and fluff up around the fenugreek leaves.
6. Keep stirring and remove from heat whilst eggs are still soft and fluffy.
7. Serve on hot buttered toast or in a pitta pocket.

SHAKSHUKA
~ MEDITERRANEAN ~

Eggs in a savoury tomato sauce is a popular and common dish in the Mediterranean, parts of the Middle East, and some North African countries such as Egypt. Though often consumed as a breakfast dish, it is substantial enough to be a main course and is generally accompanied by hummus and salad.

INGREDIENTS
1 red capsicum, finely chopped
1 yellow/green capsicum, finely chopped
1 small onion, finely chopped
4-6 cloves garlic, finely chopped
3 tbsp vegetable oil
1 tsp sugar
A small bunch of parsley, finely chopped
1 tsp paprika
200 gms (canned) tomatoes, chopped
1 tsp red chilli flakes
2-3 eggs
Salt & pepper to taste
Feta cheese (optional)
Crusty bread roll or warmed pitta

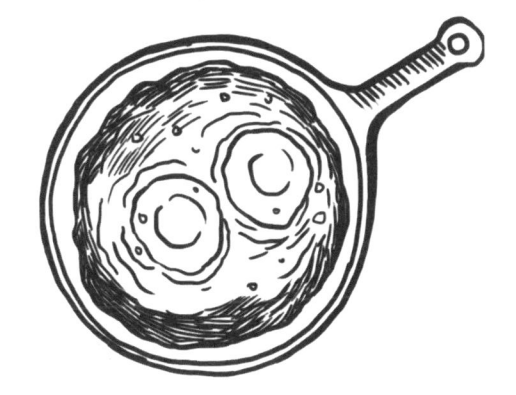

METHOD
1. Warm the oil in a heavy-bottomed saucepan. Add the onions, peppers and garlic and sauté until they are soft but not brown.
2. Add in the chopped tomatoes, paprika, chilli flakes, salt and sugar. Stir and then simmer over low-medium heat for 10-15 minutes, stirring occasionally, until the mixture becomes a thick but still runny sauce.
3. With the back of a spoon, create a couple of shallow dips in the sauce and crack the eggs into these dips. Do not stir. Cover and cook for 3-4 minutes until the egg yolks become semi-firm.
4. Remove from heat, sprinkle with the parsley and crumbled feta cheese (if using). Serve with either some crusty bread or warmed pitta pieces.

NOTES
- ➢ This is the general traditional recipe which can be varied by including different vegetables e.g. baby sweet corn, spinach, etc.
- ➢ To increase the protein content of the dish you can also include some beans e.g. white beans such as cannellini would look good in the red tomato sauce.

TOAST WITH SPINACH
~ USA ~

This makes for a healthy and tasty brunch. Followed by almond croissants, it sets one up for the day.

INGREDIENTS
1 wholemeal/any good quality, large loaf bread
¼ kg cheddar cheese, finely sliced
¾ kg spinach
1 tbsp butter
6 tbsp almond flakes, toasted
Salt & pepper to taste

METHOD
1. Roughly chop the spinach and cook on low heat for 5-6 minutes. Drain the liquid and mix in the butter, salt and pepper.
2. Cut 6 medium slices of bread and toast them.
3. Spread the toasts on a tray and then evenly cover them with cheese slices.
4. Gently spoon equal amounts of hot spinach onto each toast. Sprinkle with almond flakes to serve.

NOTES
- ➢ The spinach can be prepared well in advance and warmed up just before putting onto the toasts.
- ➢ The spinach can be replaced with mushroom or roasted capsicum.

VEGETARIAN FRITTATA
~ ITALY ~

Frittata, a baked egg dish, can be made with seasonal or leftover vegetables. It makes a hearty weekend breakfast or brunch dish and works well for picnics and lunch boxes, as it is easy to carry and is equally delicious hot or cold. It is fairly similar to the Spanish Tortilla, which is normally made with potatoes.

INGREDIENTS
8 eggs
4 stalks spring onions, sliced into fine rings
3-4 cloves garlic, finely chopped
500 gms combination vegetables, cut into same size for even cooking
125 ml single cream
½ cup grated parmesan cheese
1 cup finely chopped parsley
2 tbsp vegetable oil
1/3 cup butter
Salt to taste

METHOD
1. Whisk together the eggs, cream, salt, pepper and cheese in a bowl. Stir in the parsley.
2. In a large, oven-proof frying pan, heat oil and butter on medium-high heat and sauté the garlic and vegetables you are using. Cook until soft and nearly cooked.
3. Pour the egg mixture over the vegetables and cook on low-medium heat. Stir gently to ensure the egg mixture flows between the vegetables. Allow it to cook undisturbed till half set.
4. Now place the saucepan in an oven preheated to 180° C, for 15-20 minutes. Once the frittata begins to turn a light golden brown and has puffed up somewhat, it can be removed.
5. Use a spatula or flat wooden spoon to free the frittata from the pan and slide onto a serving platter. Cut into wedges and serve with a green salad and bread rolls.

NOTE
➢ Any fast cooking vegetable (broccoli, spinach, peppers, mushrooms) works best.

SNACKS & TID-BITS
While the recipes in this section make ideal tea/coffee-time snacks, they serve equally well as nibbles with pre-dinner drinks.

CHEESE ON TOAST
~ EUROPE ~

Cheese-on-Toast is always a delicious bite, but when hungry, tired and in need of comfort, it is most gratifying.

INGREDIENTS
Thick slices of bread
¼ cup grated mature cheddar cheese, per slice
Butter
Crushed black pepper

METHOD
1. Toast the slice/s of bread and butter it/them generously.
2. Sprinkle some pepper on the toasts and then the cheese.
3. Place the toast/s under a hot grill and remove when the cheese starts to bubble. It is delicious on its own or with a salad.

NOTES
- You can jazz up this basic recipe by adding slices of onion and tomato before spreading the cheese.
- You can also spread onion rings on top of the cheese before grilling.
- Instead of pepper, try using green chilli on top of the cheese and then grill. It is delectable.

CHOCOLATE-MARZIPAN TART
~ EUROPE ~

This is a short cut for making individual chocolate truffles. Instead of using pastry as a base, marzipan is used to make it more flavoursome and nutritious.

INGREDIENTS
250 gms marzipan (the higher the almond content the better)
400 gms dark chocolate
Finely grated rind of 1 orange
¼ cup fresh orange juice
1 tbsp rum/cognac
2 tbsp thick cream
1 tsp butter

METHOD
1. Smear the rolling board and the rolling pin with butter.
2. Pat the marzipan into a ball then roll out round to cover a 22 cm baking dish.
3. Chop the chocolate and melt it in the microwave oven (takes around minute and a half). Else place the chocolate pieces in a small pot. Fill a bigger pot to ¼ level with water, bring it to boil and turn the heat off. Place the chocolate pot over the boiled water and stir till the chocolate melts.
4. Gently mix in remaining ingredients in the melted chocolate.
5. Pour the mix over the marzipan and leave to set.
6. Cut to desired size and serve with coffee.

DATE & NUT ROLL
~ UK ~
A sweet cannot get healthier than this – it is simply natural!

INGREDIENTS
½ cup rolled oats, dry roasted
1 cup dates
½ cup figs
¼ cup almonds, roasted
¼ cup sesame seeds, roasted
¼ cup sunflower seeds, roasted
¼ cup hazelnuts, roasted
¼ cup water

METHOD
1. Pound the almonds and hazelnuts into a gritty mix.
2. Put the dates, figs and water into a good-sized pot and place on medium heat. Bring to the boil.
3. While still hot, pulp the fruit with a masher and thoroughly blend in all the other ingredients.
4. Once cool, empty onto a smooth surface and make a thick, long roll. Chop slices of the desired thickness OR roll into balls of the desired size.

NOTE
➢ For a zesty flavour, add in a handful of mixed peel.

GRIDDLE CAKES
~ UK ~

Griddle cakes are smaller and thicker versions of pancakes. Usually plain flour is used for making these. But to give the item a healthier twist oatmeal has been used. These make a very tasty coffee/ tea time snack.

INGREDIENTS (*for approx 6 cakes*)
1 cup oatmeal
1¼ cups hot water/milk
¼ cup almonds, roughly ground
¼ cup sugar
½ tsp baking powder
½ tsp ground cardamom/cinnamon/nutmeg
4 tbsp melted butter
A pinch of salt

METHOD
1. Place all the dry ingredients into a bowl and slowly mix in the water/milk and 1 spoon of butter. Set aside for 5 minutes to soak.
2. Heat a griddle/shallow frying pan and spread some butter in the centre. Place 1½ tablespoons of thick batter on top of the hot butter and fry for 30 seconds.
3. Pour a little butter on top (the uncooked side), and flip the cake over. Remove from the pan. Both sides should be nicely browned.
4. Repeat the process till all the batter is finished (should make at least 6 cakes).
5. Serve hot or cold, on their own or with a dollop of cream and jam on the side.

NOTES
- Desiccated coconut can be used instead of almonds.
- The batter can be made using water and yoghurt or a mix of half the water and 1 egg.
- Half a cup of mashed banana can be used instead of sugar.
- Half a cup of blueberries can be used in the mix for added flavour and nutritional value.

LATKAS
~ GERMANY/ISRAEL ~

Latka is a common Jewish dish in most European countries, as well as in Israel. In Germany, it is invariably served with apple sauce.

INGREDIENTS
2 large potatoes, peeled
1 medium-sized onion, grated
½ cup plain flour
½ tsp baking powder
Salt & pepper to taste
Oil for shallow frying

METHOD
1. Grate the potatoes and drain the liquid. Squeeze out as much moisture as possible with your hands or using a kitchen towel.
2. In a large bowl mix in all the ingredients and blend well.
3. Form palm-size *latkes*. In a large frying pan, heat some oil and fry them on both sides over medium heat, until golden.
4. Serve hot with apple sauce and/or sour cream with chives.

NOTE
➢ These can be made in advance and warmed before serving.

MOGO (CASSAVA) WITH COCONUT MILK
~ KENYA ~

INGREDIENTS
500 gms frozen *mogo*, cut into chips if not pre-cut
300 ml coconut milk
1-2 green chillies, finely chopped
1 tsp black pepper
Salt to taste
A sprinkling of fresh coriander
Lemon/lime juice to taste

METHOD
1. Boil the mogo chips until just tender.
2. In the meantime, gently warm the coconut milk on low-medium heat.
3. Add in the chilli, salt and black pepper to the coconut milk and simmer for 5-7minutes on low heat until the milk has slightly thickened.
4. Add the boiled and drained mogo chips to the coconut milk.
5. Stir gently and cook for a few minutes until the coconut sauce is thick and has coated the chips.
6. Serve sprinkled with lemon/lime juice and coriander.

OAT SCONES
~ SCOTLAND ~

These oatmeal scones are a healthier version of the popular potato scones. In Scotland, this popular snack is eaten with butter and jam.

INGREDIENTS
2 cups fine oats
1 large potato, boiled, peeled & mashed
4 tbsp oil
1 tbsp dry oregano
Salt & pepper to taste
1 cup water
¼ cup wholemeal flour, for rolling the scones

METHOD
1. Place all dry ingredients into a large bowl and mix.
2. Add the mashed potato and oil and blend with the dry ingredients.
3. Make a dip in the centre of the mixture. *Adding a little water at a time,* knead into a springy dough.
4. Place the dough in a plastic bag and leave it in a warm place for half an hour.
5. Divide the dough into 8-10 portions and form into balls.
6. Coat the balls with some flour. Using a thick rolling pin, roll into round or square shapes (approx. 2-3 mm thick).
7. Heat a griddle pan over medium heat and roast the scones for 45-60 seconds, till nicely browned.
8. Flip the scones over and roast for the same time, gently pressing with a spatula. Repeat the process till all the scones are done.
9. Serve hot with cream cheese and pineapple relish or butter and jam.

NOTES
➤ The scones can also be made with a finely chopped onion.
➤ Green chilli can be added for extra taste and flavour.
➤ The scones can be served with accompaniments of your choice.

SAVOURY MUFFINS
~ EUROPE ~

Europeans love sweets of all kinds. However, with growing health awareness, alternatives have begun to make an appearance as well. These savoury muffins make a nice tea-time snack or a light lunch along with a salad.

INGREDIENTS
1½ cups self-raising flour
1½ cups oatmeal
1½ cups oil
3 eggs
1½ cups grated mature cheddar cheese
1½ cups grated white radish
1 tbsp dry oregano
1 tbsp horseradish sauce
1 tsp baking powder
Salt & pepper to taste
Extra oil for greasing baking trays

METHOD
1. In a large bowl, beat the oil and eggs together till fluffy.
2. Using a wooden spoon, gently mix in the flour and oats.
3. Add the baking powder, salt, pepper, oregano and horseradish sauce and blend into the dough.
4. Mix in the cheese and radish. Ensure everything is well combined.
5. Grease two muffin/cup trays (6 cups in each). Fill each cup ¾ full with batter. Place the trays in a preheated oven (200° C) and bake for 20 minutes till the muffin tops are nicely browned. Check they are done by piercing with a skewer. It should come out clean. If not, leave for a few more minutes. Once cool, remove the muffins from the trays and store in a tin box.

NOTES
➢ If muffin trays are not available then the mix can be baked in a cake tin for 30-35 minutes.
➢ Various combinations can be tried: e.g. nuts, olives, sun dried tomatoes.

SNACKS & TIDBITS

SPINACH DROPS
~ UK ~

This preparation makes a tasty and healthy tea-time snack.
It can also be served as a tid-bit with drinks.

INGREDIENTS
1 cup self-raising flour
1 cup grated mature cheddar
1 cup pre-cooked spinach, cooled & drained
½ cup sesame seeds
1 tbsp dry oregano
Salt & crushed black pepper to taste
¼ cup oil

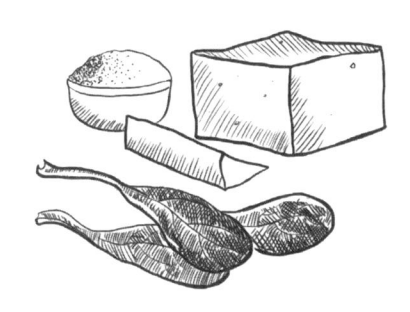

METHOD
1. Grease an oven tray with oil.
2. Sift the flour into a large mixing bowl and put in all the other ingredients. Using a fork, gently blend the ingredients into a dough.
3. Using a spoon or your fingers, place spoon-sized drops on the greased tray (12-16). Place the tray in a medium oven and cook for 12-15 minutes till the drops are brown. Serve hot.

NOTE
➢ The spinach can be replaced with a cup of cooked corn kernels or another vegetable of choice.

SNACKS & TIDBITS

WELSH RAREBIT
~ UK ~

This is a more sophisticated and calorific version of cheese-on-toast. It is also a little more complicated. However, the end result is scrumptious. It can be served for a brunch/ light lunch or in bite-sized pieces as a cocktail snack.

INGREDIENTS
4 thick bread slices
5 tbsp butter
1 tsp plain flour
½ cup milk
1½ tbsp granulated/paste mustard
1¼ cups grated mature cheddar/any other strong cheese
¼ cup fresh/1 tbsp dried basil/herb of choice

METHOD
1. Melt 1 tbsp butter in a pan over low heat. Add the flour and stir for a few seconds.
2. Add in the milk and bring it to a boil, stirring continuously.
3. Stir in ¾ cup cheese, the herb and mustard, and leave to cool.
4. Butter the bread on both sides and toast (both sides) under a hot grill.
5. Divide the cheesy mix into 4 portions and spread on each toast.
6. Sprinkle the remaining cheese over the toasts. Place under a hot grill till they bubble and brown.
7. Serve hot with a salad.

NOTE
➢ This dish can be embellished by grilling the Rarebit with tomato or onion or capsicum on top.

SNACKS & TIDBITS

LUNCH & DINNER

This section provides an entire range of soups, starters, mains, side dishes, salads and desserts. A complementary selection from each group will give you the perfect meal. Many of the dishes can be served on their own as a light meal as well.

Soups

BORI-BORI SOUP
~ PARAGUAY ~

Paraguayans tend to be meat eaters. Mangoes, avocadoes and vegetables grow in abundance but are scantily used. However, some traditional recipes survive, like this light and delicious soup, packed with a variety of flavours.

INGREDIENTS
For the Soup
1 cup finely chopped green beans (any variety)
1 cup finely chopped potatoes
2 cups finely chopped mix of vegetables
  (capsicum, carrot, zucchini, cauliflower)
1 large red onion, finely chopped
1 tbsp finely chopped garlic
Salt & roughly ground pepper to taste
4 cups water
6 tbsp olive oil
½ cup finely chopped fresh parsley
For the Dumplings
1 cup fine cornflour
1 cup grated mature cheddar cheese
1 tbsp dry oregano
1 tsp pepper

METHOD
Dumplings
1. Mix all the ingredients in a bowl and knead into a dough (add a little milk/water if too dry).
2. Leave the dough covered with a plastic sheet for ½ hour, then make marble-sized rounds.

Soup
1. Heat oil in a large pan and fry the onions till golden. Stir in all the vegetables and garlic. Toss for a few minutes, then add water, salt and pepper and bring to a boil.

2. Lower the heat to minimum and gently drop in the dumplings. Leave the soup to simmer for 15-20 minutes. Sprinkle with parsley and serve. Because of the dumplings, no bread is required.

BROCCOLI & BLUE CHEESE SOUP
~ EUROPE ~

Soup is a staple food in Europe, particularly in winter. This one is rich and creamy. The blue cheese adds a zing.

INGREDIENTS
1 medium-sized broccoli, washed & broken into florets
1 large onion, chopped into chunky pieces
½ cup crumbled blue cheese
3 cups water
1 cup milk
Salt & pepper to taste
1 sprig rosemary

METHOD
1. Place all the ingredients (except cheese), in a large pan. Bring to a boil on high heat. Lower the heat and simmer for another 5-7 minutes till the broccoli is tender.
2. Remove the rosemary sprig and blend the mixture into a gritty paste using a whisk.
3. Add the cheese and then remove from heat.
4. Serve hot with warm crusty bread.

NOTES
➤ Blue cheese is not to everyone's taste. It can be replaced with any other crumbly cheese.
➤ The cheese in this soup can be substituted with sunflower seeds. Simply add ¾ cup of sunflower seeds together with all the other ingredients. This makes for a healthy option.

CHICKPEA & VEGETABLE CATALAN SOUP
~ SPAIN ~

Catalan soups are thick and hearty and often made using pork, sausages or fish. This vegetarian version is just as delicious and flavoursome.

INGREDIENTS
4 tbsp olive oil
400 gms (2 cans) chickpeas, drained & rinsed
200 gms fresh tomatoes, roughly chopped
2 tbsp tomato purée
2 carrots, finely chopped
2 stalks celery, finely chopped
1 large onion, finely chopped
1 medium-sized potato, grated
4-6 cloves garlic, finely chopped
1 tsp smoked paprika
1 tsp red chilli flakes
1-1½ litres freshly boiled water
Salt & pepper to taste
Chopped parsley for sprinkling

METHOD
1. Heat the oil in a large saucepan over low-medium heat and sauté the carrots, onion, celery and potato until soft but not brown.
2. Add the garlic, smoked paprika, chilli flakes, salt and pepper. Stir and sauté for a minute.
3. Add in the chopped tomatoes and tomato purée. Stir, cover and cook till the tomatoes have softened and blended in with the rest of the mixture.
4. Add in half the chickpeas and the water. Simmer for 5 minutes.
5. Remove from heat, blend and purée the soup using a hand-held blender or food processor. Put this pureéd soup back on low heat.
6. In a separate bowl, mash the remaining chickpeas roughly so they are broken but retain their texture. Add to the soup and simmer for 5 minutes. The soup should be thick but runny. Simmer on high heat if too thin or add hot water if it is too thick. Ladle into soup bowls and sprinkle with chopped parsley. Serve with crusty bread.

GARLIC & PAPRIKA SOUP
~ SPAIN ~

Spaniards use plenty of paprika in their cooking which gives the dishes a vibrant red colour and zesty taste. This quick and simple recipe is ideal for a flavoursome, light bite or a punchy starter. It is usually served with a poached egg but you can substitute with any boiled/canned white beans.

INGREDIENTS
2 tbsp smoked paprika
2 slices old bread, torn into rough chunks
4-6 cloves garlic, finely sliced
3 tbsp oil
1 litre water, freshly boiled
Salt & pepper to taste
1 egg/150 gms white cannellini beans

METHOD
1. Heat the oil in a large saucepan over medium heat and add the sliced garlic. Reduce heat to low and sauté until just lightly brown. Add the smoked paprika and sauté for a minute. Add the hot water and let it simmer for about 4-5 minutes.
2. Add in the chunks of stale bread. As soon as the bread softens and the soup is simmering gently, break in an egg or add the cooked white beans. Wait till the egg is almost cooked but the yolk is still slightly soft. If using beans, simmer for 5 minutes. Season and serve in soup bowls with a drizzle of olive oil.

NOTE
➢ You can experiment with different breads. For clean flavours, white bread is best.

GAZPACHO
~ SPAIN ~

This is a thick, refreshing, cold summer soup that requires no cooking, just the blending of fresh vegetables. It is delicious as a starter or for brunch.

INGREDIENTS
For the Soup
8 large ripe tomatoes, roughly chopped
1 large cucumber, peeled & roughly chopped
1 tbsp chives, finely chopped
1-2 cloves garlic, peeled & roughly chopped
4 tbsp olive oil
2 tbsp sherry/red wine vinegar/lemon juice
For the Garnish
1 ripe avocado, peeled & diced into ½ cm pieces
1 small red/yellow pepper, diced into ½ cm pieces

METHOD
1. Combine all the soup ingredients and blend into a smooth purée.
2. Taste and adjust the seasoning if necessary. It should taste semi-sweet, a little tangy, with hints of garlic and balanced with salt.
3. It should be of soup consistency. If it is too thick, add a few spoonfuls of iced water.
4. Cover and chill in the refrigerator for at least an hour, more if possible.
5. Ladle into chilled soup bowls and serve with a scattering of avocado and pepper.

LEEK WITH POTATOES
~ EUROPE ~

This is a really decadent soup with loads of butter – so creamy and comforting.

INGREDIENTS
2 large potatoes
2 stalks leek
150 gms butter
1 tsp dry oregano
4 cups water
Salt & pepper to taste

METHOD
1. Peel and chop the potatoes into chunky pieces.
2. Wash and chop leek into chunky pieces.
3. Place all ingredients (except butter), into a large pot and place on heat and bring to a boil. Then lower the heat to minimum and cook for 7-10 minutes till the vegetables are soft.
4. Using a whisk, blend the mixture into a smooth paste.
5. Mix in butter and serve.

NOTE
This is a thick soup but if you prefer a thin soup, try this method:
➢ Chop the vegetables into tiny pieces. Melt ½ the amount of butter in a pot, add in the vegetables and stir for few minutes on high heat. Add in all other ingredients, along with 6 cups of water. Cook on low heat for 8-10 minutes.

ONION SOUP
~ FRANCE ~

Eating out for vegetarians is not easy in France as most dishes are meat or fish based. Though French pastries and cakes are superb, one cannot live on them alone. This traditional and popular French soup is served in every bistro and café and is absolutely irresistible. While delicious on its own, with cheesy toast, it is a delight for the palate.

INGREDIENTS
For the Soup
4 large onions (preferably red), cut into long thin slices
4 tbsp butter, solid
1 tbsp corn/plain/wheat flour
2 bay leaves
1 tbsp dry oregano
Salt & pepper to taste
6 cups water
For the Cheese Toasts
8 slices baguette/similar bread
Butter to spread liberally
4 tsp granulated mustard
8-10 tbsp grated gruyere/similar cheese
A few sprigs of fresh parsley

METHOD
Soup
1. Melt the butter in a large pan and add the onions. Cook on low heat until onions are soft and pink.
2. Add the flour and cook for a minute. Stir in all the other dry ingredients.
3. Add water and increase heat to full. Once the soup comes to a boil, lower the heat to minimum and simmer for 30-40 minutes.

Toasts
1. Butter the bread and spread an equal amount of mustard.
2. Sprinkle the bread slices with cheese and place the slices in a hot oven for 5-7 minutes till the cheese turns golden OR toast the bread, spread butter, mustard and cheese, and grill till the cheese turns golden.

To Serve
1. Pour the soup into wide soup bowls which have been warmed.
2. Float 2 warm slices of cheese toast into each bowl of soup.
3. Decorate with a sprig of parsley.

NOTES
- If you prefer a slightly tangier taste, a spoonful of vinegar can be mixed in with the water.
- For additional flavour, a spoon or two of brandy can be added towards the end of the boiling.

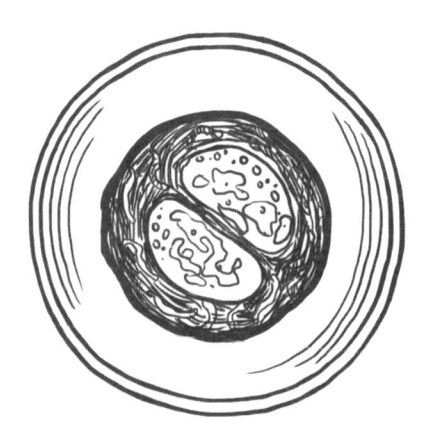

PEASANT SOUP
~ ITALY ~

As the name suggests, this is a rustic dish but also widely popular for its aromatic and nutritive nature. It is quite heavy, so with bread and salad, it is a meal in itself. It's also good for children who dislike vegetables.

INGREDIENTS
1 medium-sized aubergine
1 medium-sized carrot
1 large onion
2 large tomatoes
2-3 stalks celery
4 cloves garlic
1 cup boiled chickpeas
1 cup boiled kidney beans
Salt & pepper to taste
¼ cup fresh parsley
4 cups water
½ cup olive oil

METHOD
1. Chop all the vegetables into chunky pieces. Put all the ingredients (except oil and some parsley), into a large pot on high heat. Bring to a boil, then simmer for 10-15 minutes till soft.
2. Using a hand-mixer, blend into a rough paste of thick consistency. If using a food processor, allow the mixture to cool before blending.
3. To serve, ladle the hot soup into individual bowls, dribble oil generously, and place a few sprigs of parsley. Warm wholemeal/seeded bread for dipping completes the dish perfectly.

NOTES
➢ Any vegetable or greens that are particularly aromatic and seasonal can be added to the mix.
➢ Lentils or various beans can be used. However, the flavour of the soup will vary accordingly.

SOPA DE AJO BLANCO
~ SPAIN ~

This is a delicious and cold soup for summer, made with almonds. It is enjoyable as a starter or light brunch dish.

INGREDIENTS
For the Soup
220 gms almonds, blanched & peeled
4-5 slices white bread, preferably stale
2 cloves garlic
1-1½ litres ice cold water
1 tbsp vinegar/lemon juice
4 tbsp olive oil
Salt to taste

For the Decoration
A handful of green seedless grapes, halved
A handful of almond flakes, lightly toasted

METHOD
1. Remove the crusts and tear the bread into small chunks. Soak the bread for 10 minutes in just sufficient water to cover it.
2. In a blender, combine the remaining soup ingredients using a litre of the water. Add in the soaked bread and blend into a smooth purée with a soup-like consistency. If it is too thick, add in some more water and blend again.
3. Chill in the refrigerator for at least an hour, preferably more.
4. Serve in chilled soup bowls. Float a few grape halves and toasted almond flakes on top to decorate.

SOUP AU PISTOU
~ FRANCE ~

This hearty soup from France is delightful with a crusty roll. It can be had as a starter or for a light brunch or supper, accompanied by a fresh salad.

INGREDIENTS
100 gms green beans, cut into 1-2 cm lengths
2 celery sticks, peeled & finely sliced
1 leek, washed & finely sliced
1 medium-sized potato, cut into 1 cm cubes
2 medium-sized carrots, peeled & finely chopped
1 small onion, finely chopped
2 tsp garlic paste
2 tbsp tomato paste
1½ tbsp green pesto
1-1½ tbsp *herbes de provence* (mixture of dried basil, savory, marjoram, oregano, thyme & rosemary)
2 small tomatoes, finely chopped
440gm (1 can) cannellini beans, rinsed & drained
2-4 tbsp vegetable oil
1½ litres hot water
Salt & black pepper to taste
Fresh basil leaves, for garnishing
Olive oil for drizzling

METHOD
1. Warm the vegetable oil in a heavy-bottomed saucepan. Add in the onions and garlic and cook for 30 seconds.
2. Add in the carrots, celery and leeks and cook on low-medium heat for 7-10 minutes until soft.
3. Add in the green beans and potatoes. Stir and cook for 2-3 minutes.
4. Stir in the tomato paste and cook for another 2 minutes.

5. Add in the hot water, the herbs and the seasoning. Stir and then simmer for 45 minutes on low heat.
6. Add in the beans, tomatoes and pesto. Stir and cook for another 5 minutes.
7. Serve hot with a drizzle of olive oil and a sprinkling of roughly torn basil leaves.

NOTES
- This recipe uses pesto, which is actually an Italian paste made of basil, pine nuts, garlic and parmesan cheese. The French traditionally made their own pistou with basil, garlic and parmesan.
- As a variation, you can use red pesto instead of green – when you will not need tomato purée.

Starters

AUBERGINE WITH NUTS
~ MEDITERRANEAN ~

This preparation can be served as part of a larger mezze *or as a side dish.*

INGREDIENTS
1 large aubergine (approx ½ kg)
¼ cup finely chopped fresh mint
1 tbsp salt
1 tsp crushed black pepper
¼ cup roasted pine nuts/nuts or seeds of choice
2 tbsp olive oil
Oil for frying

METHOD
1. Cut the aubergines into bite-sized cubes. Sprinkle with salt and mix well. Leave for at least ½ hour in a colander (or tilted dish), for the water to drain out.
2. Heat the oil in a frying pan. Dab the aubergine pieces with tissue or cloth to absorb any excess water and then fry them till golden. Remove and cool.
3. Once cool, add the nuts, olive oil, pepper and mint, and mix gently with a spoon.

NOTES
- Instead of nuts, crumbled feta cheese can be used.
- Chopped green olives also add colour, taste and flavour to the dish.
- For a slightly tart taste, 2 tbsp lemon juice can be mixed in.
- A teaspoon of crushed garlic can be used for extra aroma and taste.
- The same dish can be made with mushrooms or potatoes.

BABAGANOUSH
~ LEBANON, SYRIA, PALESTINE ~

INGREDIENTS
2 large or 3 medium-sized aubergines
3-4 tbsp tahini
2 tbsp olive oil
Juice of 1 lemon
3 cloves garlic, well crushed
1 green chilli, deseeded & finely chopped
1 tsp cumin, lightly toasted & crushed
½ tsp salt
Chopped parsley and/or pomegranate seeds, for garnishing

METHOD
1. Cook the aubergines either directly over the flame on a gas ring or under a hot grill.
   To cook over a direct flame: using tongs to rotate the aubergines, cook until the skin has become scorched and the flesh soft. This wonderful, smoky flavour is distinctive of Babaganoush.
   To cook under a grill: preheat the grill to 230°C. Prick the aubergines all over and cook on a baking tray for 15-20 minutes or until the flesh is soft. Turning the tray halfway through and also turning the aubergines over, will ensure they are cooked evenly.
1. Cool for 10 minutes and then peel. Put the aubergine flesh into a bowl and mash with a fork, adding garlic and salt.
2. Add the tahini, chillies and lemon juice and mix well.
3. Transfer into a serving bowl and sprinkle with cumin and drizzle with olive oil.
4. Garnish with pomegranate and/or parsley and serve with warm pitta/flat bread of your choice.

NOTES
- Babaganoush makes an excellent starter, picnic or barbecue dish as part of a *mezze*.
- All the seasonings can be adjusted to taste.

BROAD BEANS SALAD
~ GREECE ~

INGREDIENTS
- 2 cups fresh broad beans
- 1 medium-sized onion
- 4 tbsp lemon juice
- 4 tbsp olive oil
- 1 tbsp coriander seeds
- 1 tbsp dry oregano
- Salt & pepper to taste

METHOD
1. Cook the beans in a few spoons of water over low heat till tender.
2. Cut the onion into thin slices and sauté them in hot oil till tender.
3. Mix the beans and all other ingredients with the onions and toss together.
4. Serve warm or cold.

NOTE
➢ This salad can also be served with a spoonful of thick yoghurt or crumbled feta.

CHARRED CAPSICUM
~ EUROPE ~

Because of its colour and fresh lemony aroma, this is a most inviting dish. It is usually served as a starter salad and tastes wonderful with warm wholemeal bread. It can also be served as a side with an appropriate main dish such as Bulgur wheat.

INGREDIENTS
4 large red/yellow/green capsicums
5 tbsp olive/any strong flavoured oil
3 tbsp lemon juice
Salt & pepper to taste
1 tbsp sesame seeds, dry roasted
1 tbsp fresh herb/s

METHOD
1. Rub a little oil on the capsicums and cut them into halves.
2. Place the capsicum halves, skin side up, under a hot grill and roast till the skins char (10 minutes).
3. Peel the skin off the peppers and slice them into long pieces and arrange on a plate with the different colours coming through.
4. Put the lemon juice, oil, salt and pepper in a bottle and shake well. Pour over the peppers.
5. Sprinkle the sesame and herb/s over the dish and serve hot or cold.

NOTES
- For a stronger taste and flavour, add a clove of crushed garlic to the dressing.
- Leftovers will keep in the fridge for 2-3 days. If vinegar is used instead of lemon juice, it will keep longer.

CHICKPEAS WITH SPINACH TAPA /GARBANZOS CON ESPINACAS
~ SPAIN ~

This is a really delicious Spanish **tapa** *dish, meant to be nibbled at along with other* **tapas**. *But it is so good it can be used as a side dish or even a main course. The smoky and nutty flavours transports one to sunny Spain.*

INGREDIENTS
2 tbsp olive oil
200 gms fresh spinach leaves,
 washed, drained & roughly chopped
2 cloves garlic, finely chopped
1 tbsp smoked paprika
1 tsp dry red chilli flakes
1 tbsp chives, finely chopped
Salt & pepper to taste
400 gms (1 can) chickpeas, drained & rinsed

METHOD
1. Heat the oil in a large saucepan over medium heat. Add the chopped garlic and chilli flakes and sauté till the garlic turns a light brown.
2. Add the smoked paprika and sauté for about 30 seconds.
3. Add the spinach and cook just enough to wilt the spinach.
4. Add in the chickpeas, chives, salt and pepper.
5. Stir and cook for 5-7 minutes until the spinach is completely wilted around the chickpeas.
6. Serve with warm chunky bread.

NOTE
➢ You can vary this by adding chopped red pepper, sautéed for 2 minutes before adding the paprika.
➢ You can also use fresh kale instead of spinach but kale (being a little tougher), will require about 2-3 minutes on medium heat to soften.

DOLMAS WITH ORANGE TWIST
~ GREECE, TURKEY, MIDDLE EAST ~

Preparing dolmas *is a real labour of love. You will need at least an hour (more if the vine leaves are not pre-prepared). Add another 15-20 minutes for the final cooking. But the dish is worth the time spent. Also, it can be prepared in advance.*

INGREDIENTS
30-40 vine leaves
For the Filling
2 cups boiled rice (slightly soft)
½ cup pine kernels/nut of choice, roasted
¼ cup sour yoghurt/2 tbsp lemon juice
1 large onion, finely chopped
¼ cup olive oil
½ cup finely chopped mint
Salt & pepper to taste
For the Sauce
½ cup orange juice
2 tbsp lemon juice
1 tsp sugar
For the Garnish
6-8 slices thinly cut orange & lemon

METHOD
Preparing the Vine Leaves
Depending on the size of the leaves, use 2 to 3 leaves per dolma. *Place them shiny side down.*
1. If the leaves are pre-prepared (from a packet or tin), just spread them out.
2. If the leaves are raw, trim off the hard bits, then wash and boil them in a good amount of lightly salted water till tender (15-20 minutes). Drain and spread out on a clean surface.

Filling
1. Heat ¾ of the oil in a pan and fry the onions till pink. Mix in all components in the Ingredients section (except the mint).
2. Once the mixture has cooled blend in the mint.
3. Use 2-3 leaves per *dolma* and place 1 tbsp of the filling in the centre of each *dolma*.
4. *To fold*: overlap the ends of the leaves over the rice mix first. Then, starting from the open end, roll into a cigar shaped parcel. Place the *dolmas* in a wide pan, making sure they are tightly packed together with the folded ends facing down.
5. In a pot, mix together the orange and lemon juice. Add the sugar and remaining olive oil. Pour this evenly over the *dolmas*. Place over medium heat and bring the liquid to a boil. Reduce the heat and simmer for 10-15 minutes.

Garnishing
1. Make a single cut from the centre to the edge of each orange and lemon slice. Twist the slices.
2. **Serving option 1:** completely dry out the liquid and serve the *dolmas* cold, garnished with the orange and lemon twists.
3. **Serving option 2:** retain some of the liquid in the pan and serve warm in individual dishes, garnished with the orange and lemon twists.

NOTES
➢ Dill can be used instead of mint.
➢ Instead of orange juice you can simply use ¾ cup water, oil and lemon juice, and simmer till the liquid dries.

HUMMUS
~ MEDITERRANEAN ~

Hummus is an essential part of the Mediterranean diet. It is eaten for breakfast or as a snack/ starter with warm bread.

INGREDIENTS
2 cups chickpeas, soft boiled
4 pods garlic, peeled
½ cup tahini paste
½ cup lemon juice
Salt to taste
2 tbsp olive oil
½ tsp chilli or paprika powder
A few black olives (optional)

METHOD
1. Place the chickpeas, garlic, tahini, salt and ¾ of the lemon juice in a blender and blitz to a smooth paste. Taste and add more lemon juice or salt as needed. Add a few spoons of hot water if the mix is too thick.
2. Transfer the mixture into a shallow serving dish and dribble olive oil over it. Sprinkle the chilli and scatter the olives.
3. Serve with warm crunchy bread or pitta.

NOTES
- For a slightly coarse *hummus*, mash the chickpeas with a fork or pestle before mixing in the tahini etc.
- For a creamier version, reduce the lemon juice to ¼ cup and mix in ¼ cup of thick yoghurt.
- For a nuttier version, use 1 cup of chickpeas and 1 cup of black chickpeas (*kala chana*).

MARINATED OLIVES
~ GREECE, TURKY, MIDDLE EAST ~
Marinated olives can be stored for a long time in the fridge.

INGREDIENTS
2 cups large green/black/mix of olives, non-pitted
Possible Mixes
Mix 1: 1 tbsp fennel seeds, 1 tsp chilli flakes & 1 tbsp olive oil
Mix 2: 4 fresh red chillies (chopped into 2-3 pieces each), 2 cloves finely chopped garlic, 1 tsp dry oregano & 3 tbsp olive oil
Mix 3: 6 green chillies (ready and marinated in brine), ½ a lemon sliced into small, thin pieces, 1 tbsp coriander seeds, ¼ cup finely chopped fresh coriander & 2 tbsp olive oil
Mix 4: 1 tbsp chilli flakes, 4 tbsp olive oil, 1 clove crushed garlic, 1 tbsp vinegar
Mix 5: 3 tbsp Indian pickle masala (any variety) & 4 tbsp olive oil

METHOD
1. Combine any one of the above Mixes with the olives.
2. Leave to marinate for a day.

NOTE
➢ There is no end to what one can use to create one's own blend.

OVEN-DRIED TOMATOES
~ MEDITERRANEAN ~

Tomatoes prepared like this acquire a very special taste of their own – slightly sweet and tangy with that charred aroma. They are irresistible with something like hot garlic bread. They also add colour to a mezze *platter.*

INGREDIENTS
½ kg baby tomatoes
½ cup oil
1 tbsp dry oregano
Salt & pepper to taste

METHOD
1. Turn the oven to maximum. Lightly oil a large but shallow oven dish.
2. Clean, dry and lightly oil the tomatoes and then prick each one with the point of a knife.
3. Spread the tomatoes in the oiled dish and roast for 10 minutes. Lower the heat to minimum and leave them for another 20 minutes till they have shrivelled and browned slightly.
4. Turn off the oven and leave the tomatoes for a few hours till the oven has cooled completely.
5. Place the tomatoes in a large bowl and gently mix in the remaining oil and all the other ingredients.
6. Serve as desired.

NOTES
➢ Black olives can be added for colour and flavour.
➢ This dish can be stored in the fridge for a week but add extra oil to cover the tomatoes.
➢ To save energy or if the oven is being used for another dish, place the raw tomatoes in the hot (but turned off) oven and leave them to shrivel till the oven goes cold.

PATATAS BRAVAS
~ SPAIN ~

This is one of Spain's most popular tapa *dish and combines crispy potatoes with a paprika-laden tomato sauce.*

INGREDIENTS
500 gms small new potatoes/any waxy potatoes
10 tbsp vegetable oil
1½ tbsp smoked paprika
1 tsp red chilli powder
1 medium-sized onion, finely chopped
5-6 cloves garlic, finely chopped
200 gms sieved tomatoes/liquidised ripe tomatoes
Salt to taste
A handful of parsley, finely chopped, for garnishing

METHOD
1. Prepare the potatoes first by parboiling them till soft but not fully cooked through. Then drain, cool, peel and cut them into 2 cm cubes.
2. While the potatoes are parboiling, preheat the oven to 200°C.
3. Pour 6 tbsp oil into a baking tray and pop into the hot oven to heat. Once hot, retrieve the tray and spread out the cut potatoes in it. Sprinkle half the smoked paprika. Drizzle in most of the oil until all the potatoes are coated in the paprika and oil. Bake for 30-40 minutes, turning the potatoes a couple of times to ensure they are brown and crisp all over.
4. While the potatoes are baking, prepare the sauce. Heat the remaining oil in a saucepan and sauté the onions until soft and translucent.
5. Add the remaining paprika, chilli powder, salt and garlic. Sauté for a minute or two.
6. Add the tomatoes and stir over low-medium heat. Simmer till the sauce has cooked and thickened. Taste and adjust the seasoning as necessary.
7. Remove the baked potatoes and gently cover them with the sauce.
8. Serve straight away, garnished with a sprinkling of parsley.

POTATO SALAD
~ MEDITERRANEAN ~

INGREDIENTS
6 medium-size potatoes, boiled
1 red onion, cut into thin rings
¼ cup olive oil
¼ cup wine vinegar
½ cup fresh finely chopped mint/coriander
Salt & pepper to taste

METHOD
1. Blend the oil, vinegar, salt and pepper and whip with a fork till the mixture turns thick and creamy.
2. Mix in the onions.
3. Peel the potatoes while still hot and cut them into rounds of 3-4 mm thickness. Gently mix them in with onions, etc., taking care that the potato pieces do not break.
4. When the mixture has cooled, mix in the mint and serve.

NOTE
➢ A bunch of small green onions can be used instead of the red.

Please note: the previous Starter recipes also include recipes for Mezze. Mezze is a platter of bites, served as starters in Greece, Turkey and parts of the Middle East. In Greece, it is known as mezze while in Spain it is called tapas. However, the individual items can also be served as starters with warm bread or salad on both.

Mains

AUBERGINE PARMIGIANA
~ ITALY ~

INGREDIENTS
2 large aubergines, cut into 1 cm thick rounds
400 gms (2 cans) chopped tomatoes
1 tbsp tomato paste
6-8 cloves garlic, finely chopped
1 tbsp dried oregano
1 tsp dried basil
4 tbsp olive/vegetable oil
4 tbsp vegetable oil for brushing the aubergine
1 tsp sugar
400 gms mozzarella, sliced
50 gms parmesan cheese
1 tsp dried chilli flakes (optional)
Salt to taste

METHOD
1. Heat a large griddle/non-stick pan. Brush the aubergine slices on both sides with the vegetable oil and place them in a single layer in the pan. Cook on medium-high heat, turning them over until they are soft and brown on both sides. Cook all the slices and set aside.
2. In a medium-sized saucepan, heat the olive/vegetable oil and add the chopped garlic. Let it sizzle and go a soft brown. Add the chopped tomatoes, tomato paste, oregano, basil, sugar, salt and chilli flakes (if using). Stir and then simmer on low-medium heat, stirring occasionally, till the tomatoes have been reduced to a fairly smooth and thick sauce. Taste and adjust the seasoning.
3. Preheat the oven to 200°C. In a deep oven-proof dish, spoon in a layer of the sauce. Top with a layer of the aubergine slices. Top with a layer of mozzarella slices. Grate parmesan cheese over it. Repeat the layers. Bake for 25-30 minutes till it is bubbling and golden. Remove and let it rest for 10 minutes. Serve with a salad.

BREAD GNOCCHI
~ EUROPE ~

This is an easier alternative to potato gnocchi and a creative way of using up stale bread.

INGREDIENTS
For the Gnocchi
4-5 brown bread slices
¼ cup sunflower seeds/nuts of choice
¼ cup sour yoghurt
1 tbsp dry oregano
Salt & crushed pepper to taste
Oil for shallow frying

For the Mixer
285 gms artichokes bottled in oil, drained
1 large red capsicum, cut into medium pieces
1 large onion, cut into chunky pieces
3-4 cloves garlic, chopped into small pieces
Salt & crushed pepper to taste
Finely chopped fresh parsley

METHOD
Gnocchi
1. Crumble the bread pieces and mix in all other ingredients (except oil). Knead into a malleable dough (if too dry, use a little water). Taking a tbsp of dough at a time, roll into oval shapes.
2. Heat oil in a large frying pan. Reduce the heat and shallow fry the gnocchi till golden. Set aside.

Mixer
1. Heat half the drained oil in a frying pan and sauté the onion till pink.
2. Mix in the artichokes, garlic, and gnocchi. Toss for a few minutes and add the capsicum, salt and pepper. Mix gently but thoroughly. Serve hot, garnished with a drizzle of oil and fresh parsley.

NOTE
➢ White bread also makes good gnocchi. You can use colourful seasonal vegetables as well.

BULGUR WHEAT WITH SUNFLOWER SEEDS
~ MIDDLE EAST ~

Both couscous and bulgur wheat are integral to Middle Eastern/North African/Turkish cuisines. Bulgur wheat is usually steamed and served with a gravy dish or used in a salad mix. Either way, it adds nutritional value and is a good alternative to rice. This recipe is a slight departure from the traditional method.

INGREDIENTS
1 cup bulgur wheat
1 large onion, finely chopped
2 tbsp tomato purée/½ cup chopped tomatoes
½ cup sunflower seeds
Salt & coarse black pepper to taste
2-3 tbsp dried/fresh herbs of choice
2 bay leaves
¼ cup olive oil
3 cups water

METHOD
1. Heat the oil in a broad pan and fry the onions. When pink, add the sunflower seeds and stir.
2. Mix in the tomato and simmer for 30 seconds. Add the herbs, bay leaves, 2½ cups of water, salt and pepper, and bring to a boil. Stir in the bulgur wheat.
3. As soon as the mixture bubbles, turn down the heat to low and cover the pan. Let it simmer till the water has been absorbed (approx 10 minutes).
4. Check if the wheat is soft. If not, sprinkle some water and leave it on the heat for a few minutes more. At the end of the cooking process, the bulgur should be soft but not mushy.

NOTES
➢ A cup of diced vegetables of choice can be added after the tomatoes.
➢ A cup of boiled kidney beans can be added after the tomatoes.
➢ ½ cup of pitted green/black olives can be added.

BUTTER BEANS IN PIZZAIOLA SAUCE
~ ITALY ~

Pizzaiola is a versatile Italian sauce. Traditionally served over grilled meats, it also teams well with robust beans.

INGREDIENTS
400 gms (2 cans) butter beans, rinsed & drained
1 large onion, finely chopped
1 red pepper, diced
6 tomatoes, chopped
2 tbsp tomato paste
6-8 cloves garlic paste
1-2 tsp dry chilli flakes (optional)
2 tsp capers
1½ tbsp dried oregano
12 black olives, pitted & halved
1 tsp sugar
Salt & black pepper to taste

METHOD
1. Heat the oil in a thick-bottomed saucepan and sauté the onions on low-medium heat until soft.
2. Add in the garlic, capers, pepper, chilli flakes and half the oregano. Sauté until the pepper pieces have softened but still hold their shape. Stir in the chopped tomatoes, tomato paste and salt. Cover and cook over medium heat, stirring frequently, until the tomatoes have broken down.
3. Add in the sugar, black pepper, olives and drained butter beans. Stir and simmer for 10 minutes. Add in some hot water if the sauce becomes too thick and dry. After 10 minutes the beans will have absorbed the flavours. Stir in the remaining oregano. Taste and adjust the seasoning.
4. Serve with any green steamed vegetables such as broccoli or green beans, and sautéed potatoes. Alternatively, ladle into a soup bowl, drizzle with olive oil, and serve with a green salad and some crusty bread to soak up the lovely sauce.

CANNELLONI
~ ITALY ~

It is said that Marco Polo brought pasta to Europe from China. The Italians have added many shapes and sauces. Cannelloni can be made using readymade pasta or with savoury pancakes. It requires at least an hour of preparation and 45-50 minutes cooking time. It makes a rich meal and is best served with a light, crunchy salad.

INGREDIENTS

For the Cannelloni (Pancakes)
18-20 tbsp plain flour
2 tbsp olive oil
1 egg (optional)
Salt to taste
1 cup milk/water
3-4 tsp oil, for shallow frying

For the Filling
2 cups spinach, blanched & drained
1 cup ricotta/cottage cheese/*paneer*, crumbled
1 large onion, finely chopped
2 cloves garlic, finely chopped
1 tsp ground nutmeg
Salt & crushed pepper to taste
¼ cup olive oil

For the Topping (Béchamel Sauce)
3 tbsp plain flour
1 tbsp butter
1½ cups grated mature cheddar cheese
1 clove garlic, crushed
½ litre milk
Salt & pepper to taste

METHOD

Cannelloni
1. Blend all the cannelloni ingredients (except the oil for shallow frying), with a whisk, to make a smooth and slightly runny batter (use more milk/water if necessary).
2. Heat a frying pan well and put in a thin layer of oil. Ladle in ¼ cup of the batter. Spread the batter quickly to make a thin round pancake.
3. Cook for 30-40 seconds and flip. Give this side 30-40 seconds as well and repeat the process to make all 6 pancakes.

Filling
1. Heat oil in a pan and fry the onions till pink. Add the garlic and spinach and cook for 5 minutes.
2. Add all the other ingredients and cook for 5 minutes. Leave to cool.

Topping
1. Mix the flour with some water to make a smooth (slightly runny) paste.
2. Place the milk in a good-sized pan over medium heat.
3. Add the butter. As soon as it melts, blend in the flour paste and increase the heat to full. Keep stirring so *no* lumps form in the béchamel sauce.
4. Mix in all the other ingredients and add ¼ of the cheese. Keep stirring till the cheese melts. Ensure the sauce remains smooth and of pouring consistency. Add milk if required.

And finally...
1. Spread out the pancakes and place equal amounts of the filling in the centre of each (*if using readymade tubes, simply fill them with equal amounts of filling*).
1. Roll the pancakes tight and place them on a well greased tray.
2. Pour the béchamel sauce over the cannelloni. Carefully and evenly, spread the remaining cheese over the sauce. Place the tray in a medium-hot oven and bake for 40-50 minutes till the sauce bubbles and the top browns.
3. Serve hot with a salad of choice.

NOTES
- Corn kernels can be used instead of spinach.
- For a lighter béchamel sauce use cornflour instead of plain wheat flour.

CHICKPEAS & AUBERGINE
~ LEBANON ~

This is a popular dish in the Middle East and has a delicious, robust, tomato flavour. The firm texture of the chickpeas contrast delightfully with the soft aubergine. The aubergines are best prepared separately and added towards the end in order to retain their structure and texture.

INGREDIENTS
400 gms (2 cans) chickpeas, rinsed & drained
2 medium-sized aubergines, cut into bite-sized cubes
1 medium-sized onion, finely chopped
400 gms (1 can) chopped tomatoes
1 tbsp tomato purée
6 cloves garlic paste
1-2 tsp red chilli flakes or to taste
1 tsp cinnamon powder
6 tbsp vegetable oil
Salt & black pepper to taste
A bunch of fresh parsley, finely chopped

METHOD
1. Heat 4 tbsp oil in a large non-stick frying pan. Sauté the aubergines, stirring frequently to ensure even browning. Once soft and brown, remove into a colander/kitchen towel to drain any excess oil.
2. In a large saucepan, heat the remaining oil and sauté the onions until translucent. Add in the garlic and stir. Add the chilli flakes, cinnamon, salt and black pepper and sauté. Add in the chopped tomatoes and purée. Cook for 10-15 minutes, stirring frequently until the tomatoes have softened into a smooth sauce. Add some hot water if the sauce is too thick.
3. Add the chickpeas and half the parsley. Stir and cook for 5 minutes. It should be a somewhat dry dish but with enough sauce for the aubergines to absorb. Add in the aubergines, stir gently and cook for 2 minutes. Sprinkle with parsley and serve with a dollop of fresh yoghurt, a crispy pitta and/or a green salad. This dish can be eaten hot or at room temperature.

CHICKPEAS WITH MOGO (CASSAVA)
~ EAST AFRICA ~

Mogo is a staple food in East Africa and is used in varied combinations. The coconut milk makes this a mellow and mild dish. But you can increase the cayenne pepper if you prefer a more spicy taste.

INGREDIENTS
400 gms (2 cans) chickpeas, drained & rinsed
500 gms *mogo*, frozen/fresh
200 ml heavy coconut milk
1 large onion, finely chopped
2 tbsp vegetable oil
1 tsp cayenne pepper
Salt & pepper to taste
A bunch of fresh coriander, chopped

METHOD
1. Prepare the mogo first. If using the fresh variety, peel and cut into 10 cm long chunks, then boil until just tender. Drain and cut into bite-sized cubes and set aside.
2. Heat the oil in a saucepan and sauté the chopped onions until soft and translucent.
3. Add in the cayenne, salt, and black pepper. Stir.
4. Add in the drained chickpeas and the cubed mogo. Sauté for a couple of minutes so that the mogo browns a little and the spices coat everything.
5. Add the coconut milk and stir. Simmer for 5-7 minutes on low-medium heat until a rich thick gravy has formed and coats the chickpeas and mogo.
6. Sprinkle the dish with the chopped coriander and serve with plain pitta/paratha/chapattis.

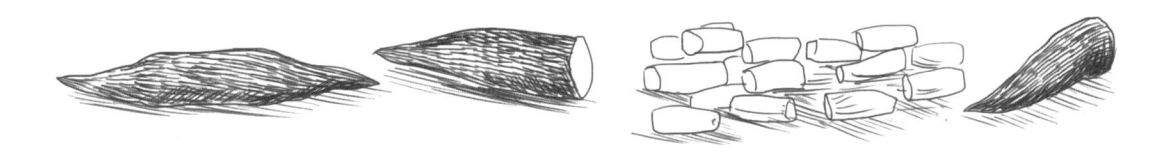

CHILLI CON QUESO
~ MEXICO ~

Mexicans use several types of beans (pinto, black turtle, red, kidney beans, etc). To make chilli, they combine beans with meat (carne). Here, cheese (queso), has been substituted, hence the name of the dish. However, it should not be confused with **Chilli con Queso,** *a Mexican cheesy dip.*

INGREDIENTS
2 cups kidney beans, boiled (retain 3 cups water)
1½ cups crumbled *paneer* or halloumi
2 tbsp tomato purée
1 large onion, finely chopped
2 cloves garlic, finely chopped
2-3 bay leaves
1 tbsp coriander seeds
1 tbsp dry oregano
½ tsp chilli powder
½ tsp crushed chilli/to taste
Salt to taste
½ cup oil

METHOD
1. In a good-sized pan, heat the oil and fry the onion till golden.
2. Add the *paneer* and stir till it starts to brown. Mix in the tomato purée, garlic and coriander. Stir on low heat till the oil separates. Stir in all the other ingredients and bring to a boil. Lower the heat to minimum and simmer for 15-20 minutes. Serve with boiled rice.

NOTES
➤ Tofu can be used instead of *paneer*.
   i. Healthy version: add crumbled tofu and brown it as for the *paneer*.
   ii. Less healthy but tastier version: chop tofu into tiny pieces; absorb the excess water in tissue paper and then deep fry. Mix this with all the other ingredients.

CORN-ON-COB SABZI
~ KENYA ~

Corn or maize is one of Kenya's staple crops. The Indian population there has created a range of corn dishes of their own. This one is particularly interesting as it uses corn cobs rather than just kernels.

INGREDIENTS
2 medium-sized corn cobs, dehusked & cut into 3 cm lengths
1 large onion, finely chopped
2 medium-sized ripe tomatoes, puréed
100 gms peanuts, roasted & coarsely crushed
3 tbsp vegetable oil
1 cinnamon stick
4 cloves
1 tsp cumin seeds
½ tsp turmeric powder
2-3 green chillies/to taste, cut into fine rings
1 tbsp coriander powder
1 tbsp cumin powder
A handful of coriander leaves, finely chopped, for garnishing
Salt to taste

METHOD
1. Heat a large saucepan of water and boil the corn cob pieces with ¼ tsp turmeric. When the corn has softened, drain. Extract the kernels from 2 corn pieces and crush coarsely. Set both corn aside.
2. Heat the oil in a saucepan and drop in the cinnamon and cloves. As soon as they release their aroma, add in the cumin seeds. Once they crackle, add in the onion and sauté over low-medium heat until soft and translucent.
3. Add the coriander powder, cumin powder, remaining turmeric and chillies. Sauté for just a minute.
4. Add the puréed tomatoes and salt. Stir, cover and simmer on low heat until the tomatoes are soft.

5. Add in the corn pieces and crushed corn. Stir, cover and simmer on low heat for 5 minutes. Add some hot water if too dry. Add in the peanuts, stir, and cook for 5 minutes. Adjust the seasoning. The gravy should be thick. But if too dense, add ¼ cup water, stir, and remove from heat.
6. Serve with plain chapattis/parathas.

DAIRY HEAVEN
~ UK/USA ~

This is the ultimate comfort food – soft potatoes with oodles of sour cream, cheese and cream.

INGREDIENTS
500 gms floury potatoes
½ cup spring onions, finely chopped
100 gms spinach, finely chopped
1 cup sour cream
1 cup mature cheddar cheese, grated
½ cup double cream
1 tsp nutmeg powder
½ cup pine nuts, lightly toasted
2 tbsp butter
1 tbsp vegetable oil
Salt & black pepper to taste

METHOD
1. Peel the potatoes and cut into 3 cm cubes. Boil in salted water until tender. Drain and set aside.
2. In a small saucepan, heat the butter and vegetable oil and sauté the spring onions on medium heat until soft. Add in the spinach, salt and black pepper. Sauté for a few minutes until the spinach has wilted. Sprinkle in the nutmeg and stir to mix.
3. In a separate bowl, combine the spinach, pine nuts, sour cream, double cream and cheese.
4. Mash the drained potatoes and stir in with the spinach mixture. Mix thoroughly.

5. Grease a shallow oven-proof dish and pour in the potato mixture. Bake uncovered, in a medium-high oven, for 30 minutes until the cheese starts to bubble. Serve hot.

NOTE
➢ This can be served for brunch along with vegetables (sweet corn/mushrooms), and/or a green salad.

FEIJOADA BEAN STEW
~ BRAZIL ~

A Portuguese influenced slow-cooked stew, **Feijoada** *is Brazil's national dish, usually made with black beans and fresh smoked meats. This vegetarian version uses roast vegetables to give the characteristic smoky taste.*

INGREDIENTS
400 gms (2 cans) black/turtle beans, drained & rinsed
2 medium-sized zucchinis
2 large red peppers
400 gms (1 can) chopped tomatoes
1 large onion, finely chopped
10 cloves garlic, made into paste
6 tbsp vegetable oil
1 litre freshly boiled water
Cayenne pepper to taste
Salt to taste
2 bay leaves
4 tbsp lime juice
For the Garnish
Sour cream
Spring onions, cut into fine rings
Coriander leaves, finely chopped

METHOD
1. Slice the zucchinis lengthwise and then cut each length into 2 cm thick semi-circles. Cut the peppers into 4 cm pieces.
2. Preheat the oven to 200°C. In a shallow baking tray, place the cut vegetables and drizzle 2 tbsp oil over them. Mix gently and roast in the upper level of the oven for 15-20 minutes until the vegetables are soft and charred at the edges. Turn over the vegetables mid way to char all sides.
3. While the vegetables are roasting, heat the remaining oil in a heavy-bottomed, deep saucepan. Add the chopped onion and cook on low heat till the onion become soft and translucent.
4. Stir in the garlic and bay leaves. Cook for about a minute to soften the garlic.
5. Add in the chopped tomatoes, salt and cayenne pepper. Stir and simmer on low heat till the tomatoes have broken down and become a sauce.
6. Add in half the beans and the water. Mash the remaining beans gently and add them in. Stir and simmer on low heat for 15-20 minutes until the sauce thickens.
7. Add in the roasted vegetables and the lime juice. Stir gently and continue to simmer for 10 minutes.
8. Place the *feijoada* over plain boiled rice. Top with a dollop of sour cream and a sprinkling of spring onions and coriander. Serve with a plate of orange wedges.

NOTES
- In Portugal, *feijoada* is made with white beans but you can experiment with different types of beans.
- Different vegetables can also be used, just ensure they are roasted well to bring in the characteristic smoky flavour.

GREEN CURRY
~ THAILAND ~

This is a milder version of Thai Red Curry and no red chillies are used. The focus here is on creating an aromatic, herby and mellow dish.

INGREDIENTS
For the Paste
3 small onions/shallots, peeled & roughly chopped
6 cm piece fresh galangal/ginger, peeled & roughly chopped
3 cloves garlic
3-4 stalks fresh lemongrass or 3 tbsp dry lemongrass
2 green chillies
1½ tbsp coriander seeds
1½ tsp cumin seeds
1½ tsp white peppercorns
3-4 tbsp vegetable oil
A bunch of coriander
8-10 kaffir lime leaves/3 tbsp lime juice
2 tbsp soy sauce/1 tsp salt

For the Curry
2 small Thai aubergines or small aubergines, quartered
150 gms baby corn, sliced in half lengthways
100 gms red pepper, cut into 2 cm pieces
50 gms green beans, cut into 2 cm pieces
2-3 tbsp vegetable oil
400 gms (1 tin) thick coconut milk
3-4 tbsp curry paste

For the Garnish
Sprigs of coriander
1 mild green chilli, cut diagonally into 1 cm lengths

METHOD
1. Prepare the paste first. Lightly dry roast the peppercorns, coriander and cumin seeds.

MAINS

Cool and grind into a coarse mixture.
2. Combine this with the rest of the paste ingredients in a food processor and blend into a fine paste. [This can be stored in a jar in the fridge for a few days and used as required.]
3. For this curry, heat the oil in a large, heavy-bottomed saucepan. Add the prepared curry paste. Sauté on low-medium heat until cooked through.
4. Gently stir in the coconut milk and let it warm through.
5. Add the vegetables, stir and simmer on low heat till the vegetables are soft. You may need to add a few spoonfuls of hot water if too thick.
6. Serve with plain boiled rice or noodles. Garnish with the fresh coriander and green chilli.

HAGGIS
~ SCOTLAND ~

Like Shepherd's Pie in England, haggis was a way of using up leftover meat. Poet Robert Burns, brought it to the attention of the elite in his Ode to the Pudding Race. *Haggis with neeps and tatties (parsnip and potatoes), is now served as a special treat to commemorate Burns' birthday on 25 January.*

INGREDIENTS
For the Haggis
½ cup barley
¼ cup rough oats
1 cup mixed nuts (hazelnuts, almonds, peanuts, brazil nuts)
¾ cup mix of audki beans & chickpeas, soaked
1 large onion, finely chopped
1 carrot, medium grated
3 pods garlic, finely chopped
4 celery sticks, finely chopped
1 tsp paprika
2 tsp mixed ground spice (nutmeg, cinnamon, cloves)
1 tsp ground pepper
2-3 bay leaves
2 tbsp dry mixed herbs
3-4 tbsp lemon juice
¼ cup oil
Salt to taste
For the Neeps
4-5 parsnips
A knob of butter
Salt & pepper to taste
For the Tatties
4 medium-sized potatoes
A knob of butter and salt & pepper

METHOD
Haggis
1. Boil the barley in sufficient water to soften it but still retain a bite.
2. Boil the audki beans and chickpeas with the bay leaves till soft. Drain and retain the liquid. Remove the bay leaves and crush the beans and peas roughly.
3. Dry roast the nuts and crush into a gritty mix. Dry roast the oats.
4. In a large pan, heat the oil and sauté the onions on low heat till soft. Stir in mixed spices, pepper, paprika and garlic. Fry for a few seconds and add the carrot and celery. Cook for a few minutes.
5. Blend in the barley, oats, beans and peas, nuts, herbs and lemon juice. If the mixture is too dry, add some of the saved liquid. Cook on very low heat for 5-7 minutes. Set aside to cool (this should make 6-8 large muffin-sized haggis).
6. Oil a muffin tray and fill the cups to the top with the haggis mixture. Bake for 12-15 minutes in a medium-hot oven.

Neeps
1. Scrape the parsnips and boil in sufficient water to soften.
2. While still hot, mash them well and mix in butter, salt and pepper.

Tatties
1. Boil potatoes till soft.
2. While still hot, mash them well and mix in butter, salt and pepper.

To Serve
Place the haggis on individual plates and serve hot with one serving spoon each of tatties and neeps.

NOTES
- Instead of aduki beans and chickpeas, any other available variety of beans can be used in the mix.
- Like sausages, the haggis mixture is normally placed in a sheath (vegetarian variety) of different sizes and shapes (oblong or round). It is then boiled in its sheath or roasted in an oven. However, one can use a muffin tray as suggested in step 7 to bake the haggis or an ordinary deep tray, and then cut the haggis into pieces.
- One can also shape the haggis with oiled hands and place them in a tray to bake.
- Although haggis is traditionally served with mashed parsnips and potatoes, a salad is also good.

KAFTA BIL TAHINI
~ LEBANON~

This is a modified version of the traditional Lebanese **Kafta bil Tahini**, *which is usually made with minced meat. It is replaced here with vegetables and beans.*

INGREDIENTS
3 large waxy potatoes
3 large red peppers
2 large zucchini
1 large red onion
440 ml (2 cans) any dark beans, drained & rinsed
1 cup finely chopped parsley
1 tsp black pepper
2 tsp paprika
½ tsp cumin powder
½ tsp coriander powder
½ tsp cinnamon powder
½ tsp cardamom powder
¼ tsp chilli powder
4 tbsp vegetable oil
Salt to taste

For the Tahini sauce
¾ cup tahini paste
1 tbsp olive oil
4 tbsp lemon juice
3 cloves garlic, made into paste
Salt & pepper to taste
Hot water to thin the tahini paste

For the Garnish
½ cup pine nuts, lightly toasted

METHOD
1. Chop the peppers, zucchini and onion into 3 cm lengths 1 cm wide.
2. Heat the oil in a large pan/wok and sauté the vegetables on medium-high heat until they soften and pick up some brown flecks.
3. Add in the drained beans, salt and remaining spices. Sauté for 5 minutes until everything is well mixed and you are left with a somewhat dry mixture. Sprinkle in the parsley, mix and set aside.
4. Parboil the potatoes until almost cooked. Peel and cut into ½ cm thick rounds. Set aside.
5. Prepare the tahini sauce by warming the tahini in a small saucepan on low heat. Drizzle in, a little at a time, a cup of hot water to thin the paste into a sauce. Add in the garlic paste, olive oil, lemon juice, and salt and pepper. Keep stirring till the sauce begins to simmer. Remove from heat and set aside.
6. Lightly oil the inside of a shallow oven-proof dish and place the vegetable and bean mixture as the base layer. Press down gently to flatten. Next, layer in the potato slices.
7. Now pour the tahini sauce so that it covers everything. While some of the sauce will drizzle down, there should still be a pool of sauce on the top. Sprinkle the toasted pinenuts over the top.
8. Bake in an oven preheated to 200°C, for 30-40 minutes, until the top is golden brown.
9. Serve with plain rice or naan. If the dish has a fair amount of sauce, it will go better with the rice.

KIDNEY BEANS & SPINACH SABZI
~ KENYA ~

This is a dry and spicy dish, usually made with kidney beans to increase the protein content. It is a quick and handy dish if you don't have time for a separate lentil preparation.

INGREDIENTS
400 gms fresh/frozen spinach, chopped
440 gms (1 can) kidney beans, drained & rinsed
1 medium-sized onion, finely chopped
½ tsp cumin seeds
A pinch of asafoetida
1 tsp garlic paste
1 tsp ginger paste
1-2 tsp red chilli flakes/to taste
¼ tsp turmeric powder
Salt to taste
2 tbsp vegetable oil

METHOD
1. Warm the oil in a pan over medium heat and add the cumin seeds. When they crackle, add in the asafoetida and then the chopped onions immediately after.
2. Once the onions have browned slightly, add in the ginger and garlic pastes, turmeric, chilli flakes and salt. Sauté until the paste has cooked and the mixture releases some oil.
3. Add in the drained beans. Stir and cook for 2-3 minutes until the beans and spices are well blended.
4. Add in the chopped spinach. Stir and cook over low-medium heat until the spinach has mixed in with the beans and the spices.
5. Serve with hot parathas and some plain yoghurt.

NOTE
➢ You can use any beans with the spinach. If using fresh spinach, you may need to add a few tbsp of water to ensure it does not dry out before it has blended with the beans spices.

LABLABI
~ TUNISIA ~

Although considered Tunisian street food, **lablabi** *can be a foodie's delight as it allows one to customise flavours to suit personal tastes using a wide variety of garnishes.*

INGREDIENTS
440 gms (2 cans) chickpeas, drained & rinsed
1 medium-sized onion, finely chopped
6 cloves garlic, made into paste
1 tbsp cumin powder
2 tbsp olive oil
1½ tbsp harissa paste (refer Dressings section)
Salt to taste

For the Garnish
4-5 soft boiled eggs
2-3 tbsp harissa paste, thinned to pouring consistency
1 tbsp cumin powder
1 tbsp cumin seeds, freshly roasted & ground
4-6 thick slices stale white bread, torn into bite-sized chunks
Olive oil
Lemon juice/fresh lemon slices
Spring onion, cut into fine rings

METHOD
1. In a large saucepan, boil 3 litres of water. Add in the chickpeas, olive oil, onions, garlic, cumin powder and harissa paste. Stir and let it simmer for 10-15 minutes until the sauce thickens slightly.
2. To serve, place a few bread pieces in a soup bowl and ladle the chickpeas over it, ensuring there is plenty of both chickpeas and broth to soak into the bread.
3. Guests/family can then customise their lablabi by choosing from the range of garnishes.
4. The final garnish is the soft boiled egg on top. When split, it mixes with the rest of the lablabi.

NOTE
- Traditionally, lablabi is made with dried chickpeas. If using dried chickpeas, omit steps 1 and 2 and do the following instead: soak the chickpeas for at least 4 hours and then boil in 5 litres of water, the Harissa paste, cumin powder, olive oil, garlic paste and onions, until the chickpeas are tender. Continue from step 3.

LASAGNE WITH AUBERGINE
~ ARGENTINA ~

Argentina has a large population of Italian descent (over 50%), so it is no surprise that Argentinean cuisine has an Italian penchant. This lasagne is drier and takes longer to prepare than most pasta dishes but it is worth the effort.

INGREDIENTS
14-16 sheets no-cook lasagne
2 large aubergines (approx 1 kg), sliced into 2 cm rounds
2 cup grated mozzarella
1 cup grated parmesan/cheddar cheese
3 cup pasta sauce, divided into 4 portions
½ cup oil

METHOD
1. Brush both sides of the aubergines with oil. Grill or shallow fry them till golden. Set aside.
2. Generously oil a square/rectangular oven dish and place a single layer of lasagne.
3. Spread a portion of the pasta sauce on the sheet and sprinkle ¼ of the parmesan/cheddar.
4. Spread a layer of aubergine. Repeat the layering process, finishing with the aubergine. Spread mozzarella evenly over the top and bake in a pre-heated oven (medium hot) for 35-45 minutes.
5. For neat slicing, cut the lasagne when slightly cool. Serve with a salad or preferred side dishes.

NOTE
- This can be made with spinach. Mix in 3 cups cooked and slightly salted spinach and 4 tbsp olive oil with the pasta sauce and follow the same layering process.

MAHARAGWE YA NAZI
~ KENYA ~

Many Kenyan dishes have been influenced by the Indian population who have settled there, just as Indian dishes have been adapted using local produce. **Maharagwe** *is a wonderfully spicy and savoury preparation with a hint of sweetness. It is comfort food made with fresh green kidney beans and coconut milk. As fresh kidney beans are not always available, this recipe uses the dried or canned variety. You will also need generous amounts of coconut milk from the first pressing. Failing that, you can use packaged coconut creams.*

INGREDIENTS
400 gms (2 cans) kidney beans, drained & rinsed
OR 2 cups dried kidney beans
4-5 tbsp oil
1 large onion, finely chopped
2 medium-sized tomatoes, finely chopped
2 green chillies, or to taste
Salt to taste
½ tsp black pepper
¼ tsp turmeric
2 tsp fresh garlic paste
200 ml coconut milk

METHOD
1. Rinsing the beans removes excess salt and any preservative flavours. [If using the dried beans, soak overnight, then rinse and boil/pressure cook until tender and just beginning to split.]
2. Warm the oil and add the onions. Sauté over low-medium heat until translucent and soft. Do not let the onions brown (should be a gentle golden brown and soft enough to blend into the coconut milk sauce without affecting the colour).

3. Add the green chillies and garlic and fry for about a minute. Do not let the garlic brown as it will taste bitter.
4. Add the salt, turmeric and black pepper and then the chopped tomatoes. Sauté until the tomatoes have softened and blended well with the spices.
5. Add the beans along with 5-6 tablespoons of the water they were boiled in. Simmer for 2 minutes until the beans have picked up the flavours.
6. Add in the coconut cream and simmer gently for 5 minutes. While it is simmering you can use a large spoon to gently break down some of the beans to make a slightly mushy sauce. The final dish should have the red beans floating in a slightly thick golden coconut sauce.

NOTES
- Serve with plain boiled rice as flavoured rice detracts from the main coconut flavour of the dish. Having a mushy consistency is preferable so the beans melt in the mouth. There should, however, still be some whole beans to give bite and a different texture.
- You can add in chopped red peppers to make this into a complete one-pot meal.
- Use saffron instead of turmeric – it adds a delicious golden colour and another complex taste layer.
- Use ground red peppers instead of chopped tomatoes.

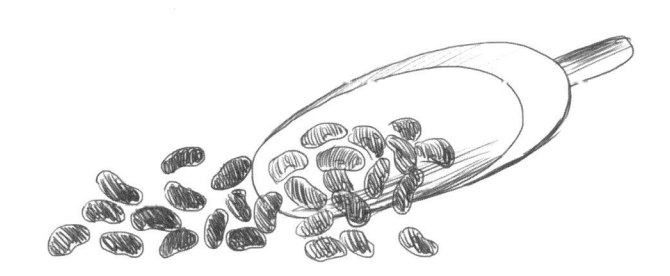

MEAL-IN-A-BOWL
~ SUDAN ~

Fondly referred to as Sudanese, *this is a quicker and lighter version of* Foul *(pronounced* fool*) or* Ful Medames *– a breakfast dish made with* fava *beans in Sudan and Egypt.*

INGREDIENTS
1 cup red lentils
1½ tsp salt
Juice of 1 lemon

For the salad
Keep all the salad ingredients in a large bowl but separate
1 large tomato, finely chopped
1 medium-sized onion, finely chopped
3 cloves garlic, finely chopped
1/3 large cucumber, finely chopped
3 crunchy lettuce leaves, shredded
2-3 tbsp chopped fresh coriander

For the Garnish
6-8 tsp ground cumin
3-4 tsp red chilli powder or flakes
2-3 green chillies (optional), finely chopped
150 gms feta cheese, crumbled
8-10 tbsp vegetable/olive oil

METHOD
1. Check the lentils for any grit, etc. and rinse thoroughly.
2. Cook the lentils in 2 cups of water at medium-high heat. Once it comes to a boil, turn down the heat to low-medium.
3. Carefully skim off the froth which keeps forming on the surface. As the water gets absorbed, add more but just enough, so the lentils cook but do not turn mushy. The final consistency should be that of a thick soup which is neither too runny nor too dry.
4. Add the lemon juice.
5. Before serving: mix together the prepared salad ingredients in a large bowl.

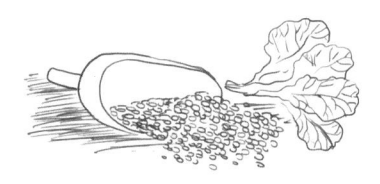

6. To serve: divide the lentils into 4 small bowls and place 1-2 serving spoons of salad on top. Garnish with 1 tsp cumin, red chilli to taste, green chillies if desired, and 1-2 tbsp feta cheese. Finally drizzle 2-3 tsp oil and serve with warm wholemeal/plain pitta bread.

NOTES
- A chilled cola drink goes very well with this dish.
- For a more elaborate meal, serve with a side dish such as Mediterranean style okra and/or Babaganoush.
- The dish can be made lighter without the feta cheese.
- A crumbly/tangy cheese works best. Therefore, *Paneer* (Indian cottage cheese), is not recommended.
- The dish can be had with other cheeses if feta is unavailable.

MUSHROOM & PARSLEY OPEN LASAGNE
~ ITALY ~

This lasagne does not require a sauce or to be oven-baked. This variation on the traditional dish is both quick and easy and the pasta simply melts in the mouth.

INGREDIENTS
200 gms button mushrooms, sliced
2-3 cloves garlic, finely chopped
1 small onion, finely chopped
1-2 tbsp olive oil
½ bunch parsley, finely chopped
Salt & black pepper to taste
3 sheets egg lasagne pasta

METHOD
1. Heat a little oil in a pan and put in the chopped onions and garlic. Cook over a gentle heat until the onions turn translucent.
2. Stir in a tablespoon of chopped parsley to flavour the oil and give a distinctive taste to the dish. Cook for a minute.
3. Add in the sliced mushrooms. Cover and cook for 2 minutes until the mushrooms are semi-wilted.
4. Add the salt and fold in the rest of the parsley. Remove from heat and set aside.
5. Prepare your lasagne sheets as per instructions on the packet. When ready, assemble the dish by first placing a sheet of the cooked paste on a warm plate. Pile on the herby mushrooms on this sheet and then drape the remaining pasta sheets over the mushrooms. Sprinkle some more fresh parsley and fresh black pepper. Drizzle with a little olive oil and serve.

NOTES
➢ Use generous amounts of parsley in this dish.
➢ You can use any kind of mild flavoured mushrooms.
➢ As a variation, you can use spinach/plain pasta sheets.

ONION FLAN
~ UK ~

An open pie is known as a flan in the UK. The method for making a flan is the same as for a quiche (France). This recipe avoids eggs altogether and enhances the taste and flavour by using yoghurt. The soft texture of the filling is an enjoyable contrast to the crispy, flaky pastry.

INGREDIENTS
For the Shortcrust Pastry (readymade pastry can be used)
1 cup plain flour
¼ cup oil/melted butter
½ tsp salt
1 tsp oil for greasing
For the Filling
1½ cups finely sliced onion rings, separated
2 large tomatoes, sliced into rounds
1½ cups grated cheddar cheese
½ cup yoghurt
¼ cup double cream
1 tbsp dry oregano
Salt & pepper to taste

METHOD
Pastry
1. Sift the flour in a large bowl and add salt and oil. Using your fingers, rub the oil into the flower till crumbly flakes are formed.
2. Adding a spoonful of cold water at a time, form a dough using a light touch. Put the dough into a plastic bag and leave in the fridge for half an hour.

Filling
1. Whip the cream and yoghurt in a bowl. Mix in half the cheese, the onion rings, oregano, salt and pepper.

Flan
1. Grease a 22 cm quiche dish with oil.
2. Lightly roll the pastry on a floured board and line the quiche dish with it. Refrigerate

for 15-20 minutes. Remove and cover the pastry with grease proof paper and fill with baking beans.
3. Pre-heat the oven to 190°C and bake for 15 minutes. Remove the beans and grease paper and bake for a further 5 minutes at 160°C.
4. Cover the pastry base evenly with the remaining cheese. Spread over the onion mix and then arrange the tomato slices on top. Bake for 35-45 minutes.
5. Once the flan has cooled and set, carefully trim any protruding pastry.
6. Cut into triangular pieces to serve.

NOTE
➢ The onion can be substituted with corn kernels (but make sure to add one finely chopped and sautéed onion).
➢ Instead of tomato, you can decorate with red capsicum slices.

PASTA WITH AUBERGINE
~ ITALY ~

This popular dish from Sicily is called Pasta a la Norma. Each mouthful gives a burst of creamy aubergine flavour along with fragrant basil.

INGREDIENTS
1 large aubergine, cut into small cubes or chunks
A bunch of fresh basil, roughly torn
440 gms (1 can)/3 medium-sized tomatoes, chopped
4-5 cloves garlic, finely chopped
6-8 tbsp vegetable oil
Salt & pepper to taste
200 gms penne pasta
Olive oil for drizzling
Ricotta cheese for sprinkling (optional)

METHOD
1. Heat 5 tablespoons vegetable oil in a non-stick pan and add the aubergine chunks. Sauté on medium-high heat, stirring frequently. The aubergines should brown all over and soften without getting burnt. Once soft, remove into a colander or onto a kitchen towel, to absorb the excess oil.
2. In the same pan, heat the remaining oil and add the chopped garlic. Let it sizzle (but not burn) for a few seconds. Add in the chopped tomatoes and cook over low-medium heat until they are completely tenderised and have reduced to a sauce.
3. Add the salt and pepper and then the cooked aubergines and torn basil leaves. Stir and leave on very low heat while you prepare the pasta.
4. Cook the pasta according to the packet instructions but leaving it just a little underdone. Add the pasta to the tomato and aubergine sauce and stir. Cook for another minute or two. Serve with a drizzle of olive oil and the ricotta cheese (if using).

NOTE
➤ A similar Sicilian dish using aubergines is *Caponata*. It differs in that it is more sweet and sour as it includes a little sugar, vinegar and capers.

PENNE WITH MOZZARELLA
~ ITALY ~

This pasta dish is rather different in that the cheesy sauce fills the penne tubes. Every quill thus oozes with sauce, making the dish succulent, aromatic and delectable. Italian cooks suggest, the longer the sauce cooks the better.

INGREDIENTS
For the Pasta Sauce
800 gms (2 tins) tomatoes
1 large onion, finely chopped
4 pods garlic, chopped
2-3 bay leaves
1 tbsp dry basil
¼ cup olive oil
½ tsp crushed red chilli
Salt to taste
A few sprigs fresh basil
1 cup grated mozzarella
For the Pasta
3 cups penne
1½ tsp salt
Sufficient water to boil the pasta

METHOD
1. Heat oil in a large pot and sauté the onions till pink. Crush the tomatoes and add them in.
2. Mix in all the other ingredients (except for the fresh basil and mozzarella) and bring to a boil. Lower heat to minimum and leave to simmer for at least 30 minutes.
3. Mix in the mozzarella and stir on low heat till the cheese melts and blends into the sauce.
4. In a large pan, boil the water with salt. Cook the pasta for 10 minutes (it should retain some bite). Drain and mix with the sauce. Serve garnished with fresh basil.

NOTE
➤ For extra flavour, dribble on a spoonful of olive oil and a sprinkling of crushed chilli.

RED CURRY
~ THAILAND ~

Red and Green Curry are two of the most popular dishes from Thailand. Red curry is hot, sour and spicy, with some sweet undertones. The coconut milk serves to mellow the fiery and spicy red chilli sauce. It is easy to make this dish at home using readymade Thai red curry paste, which usually contains shrimp paste or fish sauce, or make a vegetarian paste yourself.

INGREDIENTS
For the Red Curry Paste
1 tbsp cumin seeds
2 tbsp coriander seeds
1 tsp black peppercorns
3 shallots/small onions, peeled & chopped
7 cloves garlic
3 cm pieces of galangal/ginger, peeled & chopped
5-6 dry red chillies, soaked in hot water for 10 mins & drained
1 stalk fresh lemongrass, peeled & chopped
/1 tbsp dry lemongrass if fresh unavailable
A handful of coriander stems
2 tbsp vegetable oil
1 tsp salt

For the Curry
250 gms firm tofu
50 gms bean sprouts
50 gms green beans, cut into 2 cm lengths
50 gms fresh/frozen peas
400 gms (1 can) coconut milk
2 kaffir lime leaves/juice of 1 fresh lime
Salt to taste
3 tbsp vegetable oil

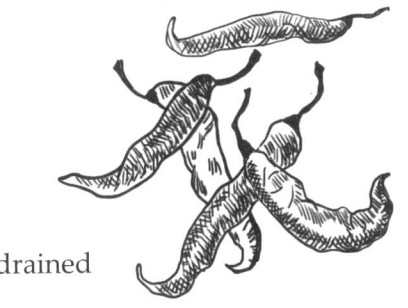

METHOD
Red Curry Paste
1. Dry roast the coriander and cumin seeds in a small pan, to release their flavours. Then grind into a coarse powder.
2. Combine this powder with the rest of the paste ingredients (either in a food processor or using a mortar and pestle), until you are left with an almost smooth red paste.
It can be stored in an air-tight jar in the fridge for a few days.

Red Curry
1. In a thick-bottomed saucepan, heat the vegetable oil and sauté the cubed tofu on medium-high heat, stirring gently but constantly to brown and crispen the tofu all over. Once browned, remove into a colander or onto a kitchen towel with a slotted spoon, to get rid of any excess oil.
2. In the same pan (which should still have some oil), add 3 tablespoonful of the curry paste. Sauté over medium heat for 2 minutes.
3. Add the coconut milk, stirring constantly to blend. Reduce heat and simmer for 2 minutes.
4. Add in the green beans and peas and simmer for 5 minutes.
5. Finally, add in the bean sprouts, tofu, lime leaves/lime juice and salt. Stir gently and simmer for another 5 minutes. The sauce should be thicker now but still quite runny. Taste the sauce and adjust salt if necessary. If you like it spicy, add a little red chilli/cayenne pepper.
6. Serve with sticky, plain, or jasmine rice.

NOTES
➢ You can try this dish using different vegetables such as pumpkin, zucchini, mushrooms or seasonal vegetables.
➢ The curry paste can be prepared in a larger quantity and the ingredients adjusted to preference e.g. adding extra or less red chillies. Remember the red chillies give this paste and the curry its fiery red colour.
➢ If you prefer a milder paste, then use milder dried red chillies or reduce the chillies, but add in a spoonful of paprika to maintain the red colour.

RIBBON PASTA WITH ROAST PEPPERS & OLIVES
~ ITALY ~

INGREDIENTS
4 red & yellow peppers
250 gm dried ribbon pasta (pappardelle/fettuccine)
12-15 black olives, pitted
4-5 tbsp olive/vegetable oil
3 cloves garlic, finely chopped
1 tsp dried chilli flakes (optional)
A large handful of parsley, finely chopped
Salt & freshly ground black pepper to taste

METHOD
1. Roast the peppers under a grill or over a gas fire, turning frequently to brown and lightly char the peppers all over.
2. Place the hot grilled peppers in a large bowl, cover and leave aside for 10-15 minutes.
3. After 15 minutes, peel the skin off the peppers and cut lengthways into 2 cm wide strips. Keep aside.
4. In a large saucepan, boil and cook the pasta according to the packet instructions. Pasta should be cooked al dente i.e. still have a bite to it and not be mushy.
5. Whilst the pasta is cooking, heat the oil on moderate heat, in a wide saucepan and add in the garlic. Stir and let the garlic soften slightly.
6. Lower the heat and add in the chilli flakes (if using) and the peppers. Stir in the salt, parsley and the olives.
7. Drain the cooked pasta and add to the saucepan. Stir gently to mix the pasta and the pepper mix.
8. Serve drizzled with olive oil and freshly ground black pepper.

NOTE
➢ As a variation, add chopped pieces of Mozzarella cheese by stirring it in after you have added the pasta to the pepper mix.

ROASTED VEGETABLE SLICE
~ MEDITERRANEAN ~

INGREDIENTS
375 gms ready rolled puff pastry
1 medium-sized zucchini
1 medium-sized red onion
1 medium-sized green pepper
1 medium-sized yellow pepper
12-14 red cherry tomatoes
2 tbsp olive oil
3 tsp balsamic vinegar
2 tsp honey
Salt to taste (optional)
Ground black pepper
Fresh basil/oregano/herb/s of choice

METHOD
1. Roughly chop all the vegetables, place on a baking tray and drizzle olive oil, balsamic vinegar and honey.
2. Pre-heat the oven to 190°C or a grill at high temperature and roast the vegetables for 20-25 minutes or 15-20 minutes respectively, until slightly charred.
3. Take the pastry out of the fridge 20 minutes before use. Spread on a baking tray lined with parchment. Score (without cutting through) a line half an inch from the edge, all around the pastry, to give a raised edge to the slice when baked.
4. Spread the roasted vegetables on the pastry and sprinkle with black pepper and salt (if using). Bake in a pre-heated 190°C oven for 10-15 minutes or until the pastry appears golden.
5. Remove and sprinkle with herbs. Serve with a leafy or crunchy salad.

NOTES
➢ Aubergines can be used instead of/in addition to the zucchini. Adjust the proportions accordingly.
➢ 50 gms grated cheddar/hard cheese, can be sprinkled on the vegetables before baking.

SHEPHERD'S PIE
~ UK ~

Shepherd's Pie is also known as Cottage Pie and has been a part of British cuisine for centuries. It is, of course, a meat-based dish. Here, mince meat has been substituted with lentils and cheese.

INGREDIENTS
1 cup green lentils, soaked
1 cup cottage cheese or crumbled *paneer*
1½ cups mashed potato (see Side Dishes – Potato Mash)
2 medium-sized tomatoes, finely chopped
1 medium-sized carrot, grated
2 stalks celery, finely chopped
1 large onion, finely chopped
2 cloves garlic, finely chopped
1½ cups grated cheddar cheese
Salt & crushed pepper to taste
2-3 fresh sprigs rosemary/herb of choice
¼ cup milk
¼ cup oil

METHOD
1. Boil the lentils with the rosemary in just enough water to soften the lentils. Simmer till *al dente*.
2. In a large pan, heat the oil and fry the onions till golden. Add the garlic and tomatoes. Simmer till soft and mushy. Add the carrots and celery and cook for a minute.
3. Mix in the lentils and cottage cheese and cook on low heat for 4-5 minutes.
4. Heat the milk and add to the mashed potatoes so it is easier to spread.
5. Transfer the lentils mix into a greased oven-proof dish. Carefully spread the mash to cover the lentils.
6. Sprinkle the cheese over the mash (can also be blended into the mash and scored with a fork). Bake in a hot oven for 10-15 minutes till the cheese browns. Serve hot with a salad.

NOTE
➢ Instead of carrot, a cup of peas or a cup of mixed vegetables, can be used.

SOPA PARAGUAY
~ PARAGUAY ~

Corn/maize and cassava are staple produce in Paraguay and extensively used in their cuisine, but rarely for vegetarian items. Although the name suggests a soup, it is more like a savoury cake. This is a basic and popular vegetarian dish, the other being chipa *made with cassava. Sopa works as a snack with drinks or as a main meal with a salad and side dishes.*

INGREDIENTS
2 cups fine corn flour
2 cups fresh corn kernels, boiled soft (can use tinned/frozen)
1 cup grated strong cheese
½ cup medium-sized cubed strong cheese
1 large onion, finely chopped
2 eggs, well beaten
1 cup milk
1 cup oil
Salt & roughly ground pepper to taste

METHOD
1. Using ¼ of the oil, fry the onions till golden and set aside.
2. Blitz 1½ cups corn kernels in a liquidiser to make a smooth paste (use a little milk if needed).
3. Mix all the ingredients (including the onions and the remaining corn kernels), to make a batter.
4. Pour the mixture into an oiled or lined baking tray. Bake for 35-40 minutes in a medium, pre-heated oven. The top should turn golden brown and be springy to the touch.
5. Using a skewer, check if the sopa has cooked through (the skewer will come out clean). If not, cover the tray with a foil sheet and bake for another 10 minutes.
6. Leave to cool for 10 minutes. Cut into square pieces and serve with drinks or as a meal with sides.

NOTES
➢ Aubergine with Mozzarella or Mushrooms in Cream complement the Sopa well as side dishes.
➢ Leftovers can be frozen and used when needed.

SPINACH WITH COCONUT MILK & PEANUTS
~ EAST AFRICA ~

INGREDIENTS
200 gms frozen/fresh spinach, chopped
400 gms (½ can) thick coconut milk
1 large onion, finely chopped
4 cloves garlic, made into paste (optional)
1 large tomato, finely chopped
100 gms raw peanuts, roughly ground
3 tbsp vegetable oil
1 tsp red chilli flakes/1 green chilli, finely chopped
Salt & pepper to taste

METHOD
1. Heat oil in a saucepan and sauté the onion until soft and translucent.
2. Add the spinach and cook over medium heat for a few minutes until it wilts. If using frozen spinach, cook until all the water has evaporated.
3. Add in the garlic paste, peanuts, chilli, salt and pepper. Sauté for 2 minutes.
4. Add the tomatoes and stir. Cook until the tomatoes are soft and broken down.
5. Add the coconut milk and stir. Simmer on low heat for 3-5 minutes. The dish is ready when you can see the spinach in a runny but thick coconut sauce. Add a few spoonfuls of hot water if the sauce becomes too thick.

NOTE
➢ The coconut milk adds a delicious creaminess and can be substituted with fresh cream for richness.

SPINACH QUICHE
~ FRANCE ~

Quiche or flan is traditionally made with a generous quantity of eggs. This recipe shifts the emphasis to vegetables thus making this quiche a delicious and light meal option. It is perfect with a fresh salad.

INGREDIENTS
For the Shortcrust Pastry (Readymade pastry can be used)
1 cup plain flour
¼ cup oil/melted butter
½ tsp salt
1 tbsp oil to grease the quiche dish
For the Filling
1¼ cups blanched spinach
1½ cups grated cheddar cheese
1 medium-sized onion, finely chopped
2 tbsp oil/ butter
½ cup yoghurt
¼ cup double cream
½ tsp nutmeg powder
Salt & pepper to taste

METHOD
Pastry
1. Sift the flour in a large bowl and add salt and oil. Rub the oil into the flour with your fingers till crumbly flakes form.
2. With a light touch, form a firm dough, adding 1 spoonful of cold water at a time. Put the dough into a plastic bag and leave in the fridge for half an hour.

Filling
1. Heat the oil/butter in a pan and sauté the onions till pink.
2. Add the spinach and cook for a few minutes.
3. Mix in the salt, pepper and nutmeg. Remove from heat and allow to cool.

4. Whip the cream and yoghurt in a bowl and mix 1 cup of cheese.
5. Blend in the cold spinach mixture.

Quiche
1. Grease a 22 cm quiche dish with oil.
2. Lightly roll out the pastry on a floured board and line the quiche dish. Put it into the fridge for 15-20 minutes.
3. Remove the quiche dish from the fridge and cover the pastry with grease paper and then fill with baking beans.
4. Pre-heat the oven to 190°C and bake the pastry for 15 minutes. Remove the beans and grease paper and bake for a further 5 minutes.
5. Remove from the oven and cover the pastry base evenly with the remaining cheese. Then spread the spinach mixture and bake for 35-45 minutes, reducing the heat to 160°C.
6. Once cooked and set, remove and allow to cool. Carefully trim any protruding pastry.
7. Cut in triangular pieces to serve.

NOTE
➢ Spinach can be substituted with a mix of vegetables charred in a pan or under a grill. Ensure the vegetables remain firm.

STUFFED ZUCCHINI
~ EUROPE ~

INGREDIENTS
4 medium-sized zucchinis
For the Filling
1 medium-sized onion, finely chopped
150 gms sweet corn (canned/fresh/frozen)
2 tbsp cooking oil
100 gms cheddar cheese, grated
100 gms walnuts/peanuts
Sea salt
Black pepper, freshly ground

METHOD
Cut the zucchinis in half, lengthwise. Scoop out the flesh, to create shells.
The Filling
1. Chop the scooped out zucchini flesh.
2. Heat oil in a wok or saucepan and fry the onion for 2-3 minutes until translucent.
3. Add the zucchini flesh and cook until soft.
4. Add the remaining ingredients and cook for another 2-3 minutes. Add the seasoning, taste and adjust as desired.

Zucchini Shells
1. Blanch the zucchini shells in boiling water for 2 minutes. Drain well.
2. Arrange the shells in a shallow ovenproof dish or baking tray.
3. Fill the shells with the filling mixture and bake in an oven preheated to 190°C for 35-40 minutes.

NOTE
➢ Stuffed zucchini can be eaten as a light main meal with a side dish or salad. It can also be added as a side dish to, for example, a main meal of pasta.

TOFU, VEGETABLES & CASHEW STIR-FRY
~ CHINA ~

Chinese stir-fried dishes, cooked over high heat, are quick to make but use meat and fish for protein. This vegetarian recipe uses tofu and cashew nuts as replacement proteins.

INGREDIENTS
250 gms firm tofu, cut into 2 cm cubes
100 gms cashew nuts, halved
2 stalks spring onions, cut diagonally into 2 cm lengths
50 gms oyster/chestnut mushrooms, cut into bite-sized pieces
1 red pepper, cut into 2 cm strips
1 tbsp light soy sauce/½ tsp salt
4 tbsp sesame oil
1-2 tbsp vegetable oil
3 cm length fresh ginger, finely chopped

METHOD
1. Heat the vegetable oil in a thick-bottomed saucepan, over medium heat. Add in the tofu pieces and sauté until light brown and crisp all over. Remove the tofu with a slotted spoon and set aside.
2. In the same saucepan, add in the sesame oil. Put in the ginger and cook, stirring constantly, for a minute.
3. Increase heat to medium-high and add in the mushrooms, spring onions, cashew nuts and pepper. Sauté for 3-4 minutes, stirring constantly, until the vegetables soften.
4. Add in the tofu pieces and soy sauce/salt. Sauté for another minute or two.
5. Serve with plain rice.

NOTES
➢ Any vegetables can be used in this stir-fry but should be cut to the same size for even cooking.
➢ As a variation, you can use canned bamboo shoots instead of mushrooms.

VEGETABLES ROAST
~ GREECE ~

Mediterranean food is considered to be healthy and generously uses vegetables, beans, rice, grains, and olive oil. There is an emphasis on salads and fruits to augment every meal. This flavoursome dish is truly tempting.

INGREDIENTS
1 large aubergine
1 large capsicum
1 large zucchini
1 large red onion
2 large tomatoes
A bunch of dill, roughly chopped
A bunch parsley, roughly chopped
4-6 cloves garlic, finely chopped
1 cup grated cheddar/other flavoursome cheese
1 cup olive oil
8 tbsp cooking oil
Salt & crushed pepper to taste

METHOD
1. Chop the aubergine into ½ cm rounds and brush with cooking oil. Shallow fry or grill till golden.
2. Chop the pepper, zucchini, onion and tomatoes into similar-sized rounds. Loosen the onion slices into rings.
3. Liberally grease an ovenproof dish (*size: approx 28cm across and 2-3cm deep [square]/ 24cm across and 2-3cm deep [round]*), with cooking oil.
4. Arrange the zucchini slices at the bottom of the dish. Layer with the other vegetables, finishing with a few tomato slices on top. After each layer, sprinkle garlic, salt, pepper, dill, parsley, and a small amount of cheese.
5. Dribble a few spoons of olive oil over and across the layers. Place in a medium-hot oven and bake for 30-40 minutes (the top layer should become golden).
6. Serve with fried rice or bulgur wheat and a salad of choice.

NOTES
- ➢ Spanish Yoghurt (see Side Dishes) is also a perfect accompaniment.
- ➢ One can substitute one or two vegetables and herbs with whatever is seasonally available. The end result will be equally good.

VEGETARIAN CACCIATORE
~ ITALY~

Cacciatore is Italian for hunter and is a rich, tomatoey stew usually made with rabbit or chicken. Vegetarian versions of this dish are easy to create using any pale coloured robust beans and seasonal vegetables and herbs. This recipe uses butter beans, zucchinis and peppers. The traditional herb, oregano is replaced by fresh fennel.

INGREDIENTS
400 gms (1 can) butterbeans, drained & rinsed
1 large zucchini, cut into 1 cm rounds
1 red pepper, cut into 1 cm pieces
1 small bulb fennel, cored & finely sliced
1 large onion, finely chopped
200 gms sieved tomatoes/fresh/tinned tomatoes, liquidised
1 tsp capers
1 cup red wine
2 bay leaves
4-6 cloves garlic, finely chopped
3 tbsp olive oil
1-2 tsp red chilli flakes or according to taste (optional)
1 tbsp plain flour
Salt & freshly ground black pepper to taste

METHOD
1. Heat the oil in a large, heavy-bottomed saucepan and sauté the onions until soft and translucent.
2. Add the garlic and sauté for just a minute or so and then add in the zucchini and pepper. Sauté until the vegetables have softened but still maintain their shape.
3. Sprinkle in the plain flour and sauté for 1-2 minutes on low-medium heat.
4. Add in the beans and the fennel and sauté for another 2 minutes.
5. Add the salt, capers, chilli flakes (if using), and red wine. Stir and simmer on low-medium heat until the alcohol has evaporated (about 2-3 minutes).
6. Add in the tomatoes. Stir and simmer on low-medium heat until the sauce has thickened.
7. Serve with boiled pasta or soft polenta and a glass of red wine.

NOTE
➢ Red or white wine is traditional in a cacciatore but can be replaced by plain water or vegetable stock, although it will modify the taste somewhat.

VEGETARIAN SALADE NICOISE
~ FRANCE ~

This delicious and filling salad is usually made with tuna fish and anchovies. It is refreshing on hot days and worth adapting for vegetarians. This recipe omits the fish and strict vegetarians/vegans may wish to leave out the eggs too. The fish has been replaced with kidney beans (you can use cannellini beans or chickpeas instead), marinated artichoke hearts and asparagus spears. Enjoy the French experience without the fish.

INGREDIENTS
For the Salad
220 gms (1can) kidney beans, drained & rinsed
4 small new/any waxy potatoes
100 gms small French green beans, topped & tailed
1 red pepper, cut into 3 cm strips
1 small onion, cut into fine rings
3 eggs (optional), boiled, shelled & quartered
6-8 cherry/small ripe tomatoes, halved
6 crisp leaves lettuce (Cos/Romaine), roughly torn
10-15 Nicoise or any black olives, pitted
For the Dressing
7-9 tbsp olive oil
3-4 tbsp red wine vinegar/lemon juice
2 tbsp French (Dijon) mustard
3 cloves garlic, finely chopped
2 tbsp parsley, finely chopped
6-8 basil leaves, roughly torn
Salt & black pepper to taste

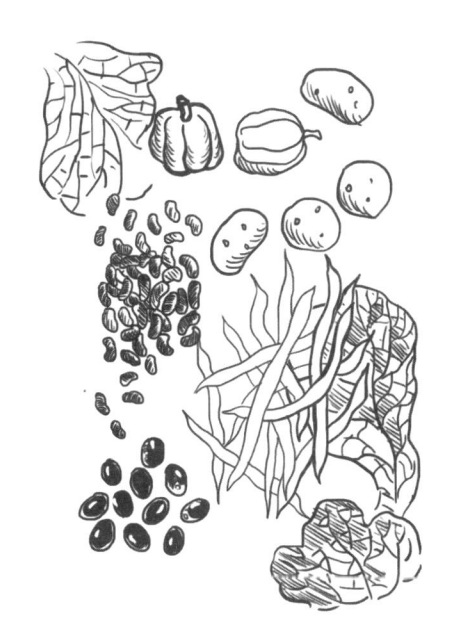

METHOD
1. Prepare the dressing by whisking together all the dressing ingredients in a small bowl. Set aside.
2. Steam or boil the green beans until just tender but with bite. Rinse in cold water to stop overcooking and to retain their bright green colour.

MAINS

3. In a saucepan, cook the potatoes in boiling water until just tender. Drain and quarter.
4. Combine the kidney beans, red pepper, potatoes, green beans and onion in a salad bowl. Add the prepared dressing, retaining a little to drizzle at the end. Toss gently to coat all the ingredients.
5. Serve the salad over a bed of lettuce and scattered with the olives and quartered eggs (if used). Drizzle over the remaining dressing. Serve with a crusty or seeded bread roll.

NOTE
➢ If serving immediately, the ingredients can be mixed at once with the dressing. If it is to be eaten later, it is better to keep the lettuce leaves separate to avoid softening and wilting in the dressing.

Sides

APPLE SAUCE
~ GERMANY ~

This sauce with its tart but underlying sweetness, can be served with most savoury snacks. In Germany, it is served with a variety of dishes and invariably with **latkes**.

INGREDIENTS
4-6 medium-sized cooking apples, peeled & chopped
1 tbsp lime juice
2-3 tbsp sugar
1 tbsp lime zest
Salt to taste
1 cinnamon stick
¼ cup water

METHOD
1. Place all the ingredients in a large pan and bring to a boil.
2. Lower heat to minimum and simmer till apples soften (10-15 minutes). Turn off the heat.
3. Remove the cinnamon stick and mash the apples into a purée. Replace the cinnamon.
4. Served hot or at room temperature.

NOTE
➢ Chilli flakes or crushed pepper can be added for extra taste.

AUBERGINE WITH MOZZARELA
~ ITALY ~

Italy abounds in vegetarian fare. In restaurants and cafes there is always sufficient choice for a non-carnivore. This dish which looks good and tastes even better, can be served as a starter or a side.

INGREDIENTS
2 large aubergines (approx 1 kg)
3 cups grated mozzarella
1½ cups pasta sauce (see Mains – Penne)
¼ cup oil
¼ cup fresh basil leaves

METHOD
1. Slice the aubergines into rounds of approx. 2 cm diameter. Brush both sides with oil and grill or shallow fry them till golden.
2. Spread the slices on an ovenproof serving dish and thinly cover with pasta sauce.
3. Spread the cheese evenly and bake in a hot oven till the cheese starts to brown (10-15 minutes).
4. Serve hot, sprinkled with basil leaves. Warm garlic bread complements this dish perfectly.

NOTES
➤ The pasta sauce can be made more flavoursome by adding a stalk of finely chopped celery.
➤ Instead of pasta sauce, slices of fresh tomato can be used. In that case, be sure to sprinkle salt, crushed pepper and finely chopped garlic before covering with cheese.

BROCCOLI WITH NUTS
~ EUROPE ~

Broccoli has its origins in Italy but is extensively used across Europe and America. This recipe makes for a high protein meal and has a wonderfully crunchy taste.

INGREDIENTS 
1 medium-sized broccoli
2 tbsp olive oil
¼ cup flaked almonds
2 tbsp lemon juice
¼ cup roughly chopped fresh parsley/coriander
Salt & pepper to taste

METHOD
1. Wash and cut the broccoli into bite-sized florets.
2. Heat oil in a wok and add in the broccoli. On medium heat, stir it around for 2-3 minutes and then add the almonds.
3. Add the lemon juice and cook for another minute. Making sure the broccoli retains its crunch. Turn off the heat and mix in salt and pepper.
4. Serve hot garnished with parsley.

NOTES
- To add colour and texture, mix in ¼ cup cooked and drained corn kernels in step 3.
- 1 pod of crushed garlic can be mixed in for a stronger flavour.

BROCCOLI WITH ORANGE & ALMONDS
~ EUROPE ~

This light and refreshing side dish goes well with hearty and robust beans-based main courses.

INGREDIENTS
250 gms broccoli, cut into 4 cm length florets
3 tbsp olive oil
1 tbsp grated orange zest
1 cup fresh orange juice
1 clove garlic, finely chopped
50 gms flaked almonds, lightly toasted
Salt & fresh ground black pepper to taste

METHOD
1. Warm the oil in a non-stick saucepan over low-medium heat. Add in the garlic and orange zest. Keep stirring and let it soften but not brown.
2. Add the broccoli florets and increase the heat to medium. Stirring frequently, cook for a few minutes until the broccoli begins to pick up brown flecks.
3. Add in the salt and orange juice. Sauté uncovered, stirring occasionally. In a few minutes the juice will have reduced and thickened and the broccoli should be tender but not mushy.
4. Sprinkle over the toasted almond flakes and serve.

CAULIFLOWER WITH POTATOES
~ GREECE ~

INGREDIENTS
1 medium-sized cauliflower (approx. ½ kg)
4-6 small potatoes (egg-sized)
3-4 tbsp tomato purée
1 large onion, finely chopped
4-6 pods garlic, chopped
3-4 bay leaves
Salt & pepper to taste
¼ cup olive oil
¼ cup chopped fresh parsley

METHOD
1. Break the cauliflower into chunky florets.
2. Parboil the potatoes and cut into halves.
3. In a large pan, heat the oil and fry the onion till golden.
4. Add the tomato purée and stir on low heat till oil shows.
5. Mix in the garlic, bay leaves and potatoes and sauté for a minute.
6. Add the cauliflower, salt and pepper, and mix well. Leave to cook on low heat for 10-15 minutes or till the cauliflower and potatoes are cooked but firm.
7. Garnish with parsley to serve.

NOTE
➢ Zucchini can be used instead of cauliflower.

CORN IN BUTTERMILK
~ KENYA ~

This dish works best using a non-creamy, tart yoghurt. Most supermarket yogurts tend to be rather mild while this dish calls for the tangy variety available in Asian shops or made at home.

INGREDIENTS
1 small corn cob, kernels removed/400 gms frozen/canned
250 gms yoghurt
100 gms plain water
2 tbsp vegetable oil
1 stick cinnamon
2 cloves
1 tsp cumin seeds
¼ tsp turmeric
2 green chillies, made into a paste
1 tbsp ginger paste
Salt to taste

METHOD
1. Prepare the buttermilk by whisking together the yoghurt and water till well blended. Set aside.
2. Heat the oil in a saucepan and add in the cinnamon stick and cloves. When they release their aroma, add in the cumin seeds. As soon as they crackle, quickly add in the corn, chilli paste, ginger paste, turmeric and salt. Stir and cover the pan. Cook on low heat until the corn is soft.
3. Add in the buttermilk. Simmer on low heat, stirring frequently. Once the sauce has reduced and thickened a bit, taste and adjust the seasoning.
4. Serve with plain rice.

CORN KHICHDI
~ KENYA ~

INGREDIENTS
2-3 small tender corn cobs, kernels removed
50 gms grated fresh/desiccated coconut
2-3 green chillies, cut into fine rings
2 tbsp sesame seeds
3 tbsp vegetable oil
¼ tsp turmeric
2 tbsp lime/lemon juice
A handful of coriander leaves, finely chopped
Salt to taste

METHOD
1. Pulse the corn kernels in a food processor until coarsely crushed.
2. Heat oil in a saucepan and add in the sesame seeds and the green chillies. As soon as the sesame seeds crackle, quickly add in the crushed corn, coconut, turmeric and salt. Cover and cook for about 10-15 minutes until the corn is tender. Stir every few minutes. The time taken will depend on how soft the kernels were. Keeping the lid on will ensure it cooks in its own juices. However, if it becomes too dry and is catching on the bottom of the saucepan, add ¼ cup of water.
3. When cooked, stir in the lime/lemon juice and serve hot with a sprinkling of coriander leaves.

NOTE
➢ This dish can also be enjoyed as a snack when cooked quite dry and served with a sprinkling of crunchy fried peanuts.

GUACAMOLE
~ MEXICO ~

Guacamole is served as an accompaniment with quesadillas but can also be used as a dip.

INGREDIENTS
3-4 ripe avocadoes
¼ cup lemon juice
3-4 cloves garlic
1-2 green chillies
1 cup green coriander leaves
Salt to taste

METHOD
1. Cut the avocadoes into halves. Remove the stones and scoop out the pulp.
2. Place all ingredients in a blender, along with the pulp, and blitz into a smooth paste.

NOTE
➢ To add extra colour and flavour, add 1 finely diced small tomato or red capsicum or both, to the basic guacamole.

MUSHROOMS IN CREAM
~ AZERBAIJAN ~

Azerbaijan having been a part of the USSR till 1991; Azerbaijani food is greatly influenced by Russian cuisine. But it also has its own specialities. Many varieties of mushrooms are found in the country, but button mushrooms give this particular dish its delicate look.

INGREDIENTS
250 gms button mushrooms
1 large onion, finely chopped
2 cloves garlic, finely chopped
1 cup double cream
1 tbsp butter
Salt & pepper to taste
1 tbsp dry parsley
1 bay leaf

METHOD
1. Melt the butter in a large pan over medium heat and add the onion. Sauté till the onion turns pink.
2. Add the mushrooms and cook on low heat till the excess liquid has dried up.
3. Reduce the heat to minimum and blend in the cream, garlic, parsley and bay leaf. Simmer for 2-3 minutes and then add salt and pepper.
4. Serve hot. This preparation goes well with something like Sopa Paraguay or fried rice.

NOTES
➢ Any variety of mushrooms can be used but larger ones will need to be cut into smaller pieces.
➢ Instead of mushrooms, three different coloured, medium-sized capsicums, chopped into bite-sized pieces, can be used.
➢ 2 cups blanched spinach is another alternative. But instead of parsley, use ½ tsp nutmeg powder.

OKRA
~ MIDDLE EAST ~

INGREDIENTS
450 gms okra
1 large white onion, halved & thinly sliced
6 fresh plum tomatoes, chopped or a 400 gm can of chopped tomatoes
2 tbsp tomato purée
2 tbsp olive/vegetable oil
1½ tsp ground cumin
1½ tsp ground coriander
1 tsp chilli flakes
½ tsp ground cinnamon
Salt to taste
1 tsp fresh lemon juice
Fresh parsley, chopped, for garnishing (optional)

METHOD
1. Rinse and pat dry the okra with a kitchen towel/paper. Trim the ends and halve them.
2. Heat the oil in a wok or shallow pan and sauté the onions on medium heat until golden.
3. Add the dry ingredients. Stir and cook for 1-2 minutes.
4. Add the chopped/canned tomatoes and the tomato purée. Raise the heat and bring to a boil. Stir and turn down the heat to medium. Simmer for 10-15 minutes until oil floats to the surface.
5. Add the okra and continue cooking till the okra becomes tender but not too soft and mushy.
6. Remove from heat and add the lemon juice.
7. Transfer into a serving bowl and garnish with parsley.

NOTES
➢ This dish can be served cold if cooked with olive oil.
➢ Seasoning can be adjusted to taste.

PINEAPPLE RELISH
~ INDIA ~

In India, pickles, chutneys and relishes are integral additions to most meals and there are myriad varieties across the country. This sweet-and-sour concoction, with the crunch of almonds, adds delight to any meal.

INGREDIENTS
2 cups bite-sized pineapple pieces (fresh/tinned)
½ cup almonds, blanched & split into halves
2 cloves garlic, chopped lengthwise
2" ginger, chopped lengthwise
4 tbsp oil
2 tbsp wine vinegar
1 tsp crushed red chillies
1 tsp dry mint/oregano
1 tsp salt
1 tbsp sugar

METHOD
1. Heat oil in a pan and add in all the ingredients and mix well. Cook on low heat for 5 minutes.
2. Remove from heat and cool. Store in an airtight jar.

NOTES
➢ This is a delicious accompaniment with snacks (e.g. oat & potato cakes).
➢ This relish can also be served with a main dish such as bulgur wheat.

POTATO MASH
~ UK ~
The ultimate comfort food.

INGREDIENTS
4 medium-sized potatoes (approx ½ kg)
½ cup milk
2 heaped tbsp butter (solid)
Salt & pepper to taste
2 tbsp finely chopped fresh chives

METHOD
1. Boil the potatoes till cooked through. While still hot, remove the skins.
2. Using a masher or fork, mash the potatoes to make a smooth paste.
3. Mix in all the ingredients except the chives.
4. Sprinkle with chopped chives and serve hot.

NOTES
- This basic mash recipe can be jazzed up by adding ½ cup of grated strong cheese.
- Instead of chives, green onions or parsley can be used.

POTATO SKINS
~ MEXICO ~

INGREDIENTS
4-6 medium-sized new potatoes
¼ cup oil
Salt to taste

METHOD
1. Wash the potatoes thoroughly and place them in a large pot. Cover with water and boil them for 10 minutes (till almost soft).
2. Remove from the water and slice into halves or fours, lengthways.
3. Heat oil in a frying pan and shallow fry the potatoes till they begin to brown.
4. Remove into an oven tray. Spread out the potatoes and sprinkle salt. Roast under a hot grill till they begin to char.
5. Serve hot with sour cream.

NOTE
➢ The potatoes can be prepared well in advance and then grilled just before serving.

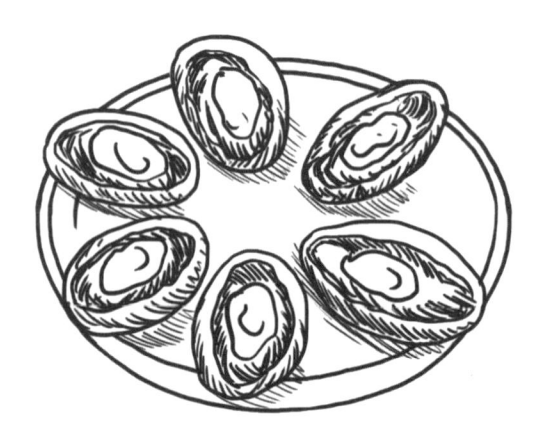

POTATOES WITH SESAME SEEDS & OLIVES
~ MEDITERRANEAN ~

INGREDIENTS
250 gms waxy potatoes, cut into bite-sized pieces
1 large onion, finely chopped
2 tbsp sesame seeds
50 gms black olives, pitted & halved
4 tbsp vegetable oil
Salt & freshly ground black pepper to taste

METHOD
1. Heat the oil in a wide non-stick saucepan on low-medium heat. Add in the sesame seeds and let them crackle and splutter to release their flavours.
2. Reduce heat to low and add in the onions and sauté slowly. Cover the saucepan, stirring occasionally until the onions become translucent.
3. Add in the potatoes and sauté over low-medium heat. Do not cover. Stir frequently to ensure the potatoes cook completely. Depending on the potatoes, 10 minutes should be enough for them to become soft.
4. Add in the olives, salt and pepper and stir through gently to mix.
5. Serve as a side dish or for brunch, along with garlic bread.

PUMPKIN WITH YOGHURT

~ AFGHANISTAN ~

Afgan food is not that dissimilar to that of Pakistan and North India. However, there are some dishes that stand out as exclusive. The vivid colours and subtle flavours of this dish are a real treat – and the taste is enticing too.

Ingredients
200 gms pumpkin
1½ cups thick yoghurt (not too sour)
1 clove garlic, crushed
3-4 cloves
Salt to taste
½ cup sunflower/sesame oil
1 tsp paprika
½ tsp chilli powder

Method
1. Wash, peel and chop the pumpkin into chunky pieces (about 2 cm cubes). Place the pumpkin in a large pot and add 4-5 spoons water, salt, garlic and cloves. Cook on medium heat for 4-5 minutes till tender but not too soft.
2. Arrange the pumpkin pieces in a deep serving dish.
3. Heat oil in a small pot and add the chilli and paprika. Turn off the heat and pour evenly over the pumpkin.
4. Whisk the yoghurt and spread over the pumpkin (allowing the pumpkin and oil to show here and there).

Note
➢ If making in advance, do so up to step 3. Before serving, heat gently (preferably microwave) and then add the yoghurt (step 4).

ROAST POTATOES
~ UK ~

The best roast potatoes are crispy on the outside and soft and fluffy inside. These are so tempting that no matter the quantity you make, it is never enough!

INGREDIENTS
12-16 egg-sized potatoes
¾ cup oil
1½ tsp salt

METHOD
1. Peel and then parboil the potatoes in salt water. Drain in a colander and gently shake the potatoes.
2. Heat the oven to medium. Pour the oil into a deep baking tray and place it in the oven for about 5 minutes (till the oil is hot).
3. Bring the tray out and carefully spread the potatoes in the hot oil. Using a ladle, scoop the oil over the potatoes till all are well covered in oil.
4. Put the tray back in the oven and roast for 15 minutes. Remove from the oven and toss the potatoes.
5. Reduce the oven temperature and put the potatoes back into the oven. Roast for 15-20 minutes till golden and crispy on the outside. Serve hot.

ROAST PUMPKIN WITH SEEDS
~ MEDITERRANEAN ~
This charred pumpkin dish has a blend of flavours – nutty and sweet, with a slight sharpness of onions.

INGREDIENTS
200 gms pumpkin
1 large red onion
1 clove garlic, crushed
½ cup pumpkin seeds, roasted
Salt & crushed pepper to taste
¼ cup olive oil
½ cup finely chopped fresh dill

METHOD
1. Chop the pumpkin into chunky pieces (about 2 cm cubes).
2. Chop the onion into long, thin slices.
3. Rub the pumpkin and onion pieces (separately) with ½ the oil.
4. Spread out the pumpkin pieces in an oven tray and place under a hot grill. Shift the pieces around after 3-4 minutes.
5. As soon as they brown slightly, mix in the onions. Grill till the onion starts to brown.
6. Gently mix in the salt, pepper, dill and garlic, taking care that the pumpkin pieces do not break.
7. Transfer into a serving dish, sprinkle with pumpkin seeds and dribble with the remaining oil. Serve hot.

NOTE
➢ The pumpkin seeds can be replaced with sunflower seeds or nuts of choice.

SLICED POTATOES WITH CREAM
~ LATVIA ~

Latvians have a way with food. Even basic dishes are served elegantly, giving them an appetizing look.

INGREDIENTS
12-16 egg-sized potatoes
100 gms butter
1½ tsp salt
½ cup sour cream
Pepper to taste
Fresh parsley

METHOD
1. Peel and chop the potatoes into thick round slices. Parboil them in salted water. Drain and mix in the butter, taking care not to break the slices.
2. Heat the oven to maximum. Arrange the potatoes in a deep baking tray and place in the oven. Allow them to roast for 10 minutes and then gently toss the potatoes.
3. Reduce the oven setting to medium and put the tray back into the oven. Roast for 10-15 minutes till just turning brown.
4. Serve hot with a dollop of sour cream and few a leaves of parsley on each portion.

SPICY AUBERGINE
~ PORTUGAL ~

This dish has a hot, tangy gravy and cheesy flavour and makes a most satisfying meal. The Portuguese like chilli in their food and their hot peri-peri sauce is a good indicator of this preference.

INGREDIENTS
2 large aubergines (approx 1 kg)
4 pods garlic, crushed
1 cup grated corvo/mozzarella/cheddar cheese
½ cup thick yoghurt
¼ cup sesame seeds, roasted
1 tsp crushed chilli
Salt to taste
¼ cup oil
¼ cup olive oil
2 cups water
¼ cup fresh basil leaves

METHOD
1. Slice the aubergines into rounds (approx. 2 cm thick) and brush both sides with oil. Grill or shallow fry them till golden.
2. Heat olive oil in a large pan. Add the garlic till a little brown. Then add the yoghurt, sesame, chilli and salt. Stir for a minute and add water.
3. Bring the mixture to a boil. Reduce heat to minimum and add in the aubergine slices and cheese. Stir gently, taking care the aubergine slices do not become mushy.
4. Simmer for 5 minutes or carefully transfer the mixture into an oven-proof pot and place in a hot oven for 10-15 minutes.
5. Serve sprinkled with basil leaves, warm bread and a crunchy salad.

NOTE
➤ The aubergine can be cut into chunky pieces if that is more desirable.

SPINACH WITH YOGHURT
~ IRAN ~

INGREDIENTS
1 cup blanched spinach, drained
1 cup thick yoghurt (not too sour)
1 clove garlic, crushed
Salt & pepper to taste
2 tbsp oil

METHOD
1. Blend the spinach with the yoghurt, garlic, salt and pepper.
2. Transfer into a serving bowl. Evenly pour the oil and serve.

NOTE
➢ 3-4 tbsp roasted pine kernels or almonds flakes can be sprinkled on top.

STUFFED CAPSICUM
~ EUROPE ~

This dish simply bursts with flavours. Its succulent, nutty texture and tangy taste, make it a perfect partner for fried rice or bulgur wheat.

INGREDIENTS
2 green & 2 red capsicums
1 large onion, finely chopped
1 large tomato, finely chopped
½ cup mixed nuts, roughly ground
2 slices brown bread, crumbled
1 tbsp dry oregano
½ cup feta cheese, crumbled

½ tsp crushed chilli
2 cloves garlic, crushed
6 tbsp oil
Fresh basil
Salt & pepper to taste

METHOD
1. Very lightly rub the outsides of the capsicums with oil. Halve them lengthways and remove the seeds. Save any extra bits of capsicum.
2. Heat the remaining oil in a pot and sauté the onions on medium heat. When the onions turn pink, mix in the saved bits from capsicum and all the other ingredients (except the feta and basil). Cook for 5-6 minutes, stirring well. Cool and divide the mix into 8 portions.
3. Fill the capsicums with the mixture and place on a baking tray. Heat the oven to medium and bake for 15 minutes.
4. Remove the tray and sprinkle the feta equally on all the pieces. Cook for another 10-15 minutes till the feta browns slightly.
5. Serve hot, garnished with basil leaves.

NOTES
- The bread and nuts can be substituted with ½ cup sprouted beans and ½ cup potato mash.
- Instead of capsicums, 8 large flat mushrooms can be used. Remove the stalk, chop finely and use for the filling.

VEGETARIAN MEDLEY
~ MEDITERRANEAN ~

One of the delights of Mediterranean cuisine is the way leftover vegetables are combined with herbs to create delicious dishes. This one uses fresh dill and dried oregano.

INGREDIENTS
2 portobello mushrooms/8-10 white mushrooms, sliced
A small head of broccoli, cut into bite-sized florets
1 red pepper, sliced
100 gms frozen corn
A small bunch of dill, chopped
Salt & freshly ground black pepper to taste
2 cloves garlic, chopped
½ tsp chilli flakes
1-2 tbsp oil
1 tsp dry oregano
50 gms feta cheese, crumbled (optional)

METHOD
1. Heat oil in pan and add in the chopped garlic. Give it 10 seconds to release its flavour and aroma and then add the frozen corn. Sauté over a medium flame for a minute.
2. Add the sliced mushrooms and sauté for 2 minutes. The aim is to quickly dry out the moisture in the corn and mushrooms, they don't need much cooking.
3. Add the broccoli and pepper. Sauté and then add the oregano, dill and black pepper. Sauté for 2 minutes. The vegetables should be tender but retain their shape. Sprinkle salt, stir and serve with a lemon slice.
4. Optional: crumble some feta cheese over the dish to add in another layer of flavour.
5. Serve as a side dish or a main course with a bread roll.

Salads & Dressings

APPLE & CELERY SALAD
~ EUROPE ~

INGREDIENTS
1 large apple
2 stalks celery
1 tbsp mayonnaise
1 tbsp lemon juice
¼ cup walnuts
Pepper to taste
¼ cup fresh basil, torn

METHOD
1. Chop the apple and celery into bite-sized pieces.
2. Toss all the ingredients together in a bowl with the apple and celery.
3. Garnish with basil before serving.

NOTE
➢ Sultanas can also be added for a sweet element.

AVOCADO & ORANGE SALAD
~ EUROPE ~

INGREDIENTS
1 large ripe avocado
1 large juicy sweet orange
1 tsp orange zest (grated orange rind)
½ cup mint leaves, finely chopped
½ cup walnuts, shelled & broken into small pieces
2 tbsp olive/any light vegetable oil
1 tbsp lemon juice
Salt & freshly ground black pepper

METHOD
1. Using a sharp knife, slice off about ½ cm off the top and bottom of the orange so it can sit flat. With the knife, peel off the orange skin and pith. Using the same sharp knife, hold the orange in one hand and start slicing the orange segments close to the white dividing membrane, with the other. Slice through on both sides of each membrane, going to the core of the orange and each orange segment will fall out. Do this over a bowl to catch all the juices together with the segments.
2. Next, prepare the dressing by whisking together the oil, lemon juice, salt and pepper.
3. Prepare the avocado last to prevent discolouration. Peel and pit the avocado and cut into long slices of similar thickness to the orange segments.
4. Add the avocado to the orange segments, toss in the walnut pieces and the mint leaves. Pour in the dressing and toss gently. Let it sit for 10-15 minutes for the flavours to mingle before serving.

BEETROOT SALAD WITH DILL
~ EUROPE ~

Finely sliced raw beetroots are used in this refreshing salad which retains their crunchiness and earthy flavour.

INGREDIENTS
4 small beetroots, peeled
1 small cucumber, peeled
¼ bunch of dill, finely chopped
2 tbsp sesame seeds, lightly roasted
100 gms feta cheese
1 tsp dried chilli flakes (optional)
2 tbsp red wine vinegar/lemon juice
5 tbsp olive/light vegetable oil
½ tsp salt
Black pepper, freshly ground

METHOD
1. Using a mandolin or potato slicer, slice the beetroots into very fine round pieces. Set aside.
2. Halve the cucumber lengthways and use a spoon to scoop out the watery seeds. Discard the seeds and slice the cucumber on the mandolin to produce the same fine slices as the beetroot.
3. Using a shallow salad platter, spread the sliced beetroot and cucumber and scatter the sesame seeds and dill over the salad.
4. In a small bowl, whisk together the oil, vinegar/lemon juice, salt, black pepper and chilli flakes (if using). Pour over the salad and toss gently to coat all the ingredients with the dressing.
5. Crumble the feta over the salad and serve.

CARROT WITH LEMON
~ CUBA ~

Cuba is better known for its music, dance and cigars, but this simple and tasty salad is well worth trying. Since it is not tempered with salt or pepper, it is tangy and fresh while being low in calories.

INGREDIENTS
2 large carrots, grated
4 tbsp lemon juice
½ cup pumpkin seeds/peanuts/cashew nuts
½ cup sultanas
½ cup chopped fresh coriander

METHOD
1. Mix all ingredients together and serve.

CARROT WITH PEANUTS
~ EUROPE ~

The sweet carrots and salty peanuts, with a hint of tang, makes an appetizing dish. It also works well in a mezze.

INGREDIENTS
2 large carrots, scraped & cut into 1X2 cm sticks
2 tbsp lemon juice
1 cup salted peanuts, roughly crushed
½ cup chopped fresh mint
Salt and pepper to taste
4 tbsp olive oil

METHOD
1. Mix all the ingredients together with carrot and peanuts.
2. Serve with crusty warm bread or as desired.

CLASSIC GREEK SALAD
~ GREECE ~

INGREDIENTS
1 large cucumber
1 large red pepper
2 medium-sized ripe tomatoes
1 large mild onion
50 gm black olives
75 gm feta cheese, crumbled
For the Dressing
6 tbsp olive oil
2 tbsp red wine vinegar
2 tsp dried oregano
Salt & freshly ground black pepper to taste

METHOD
1. Slice the cucumber, pepper, tomatoes and onion into ½ cm thick rounds. Combine in a large salad bowl.
2. Whisk together all the dressing ingredients and pour over the salad. Toss gently to coat.
3. Scatter the olives and crumble over the feta cheese to serve.

ZUCCHINI DIP

~ MEDITERRANEAN ~

This cooling dip is excellent with crudité, bread sticks, pitta bread or alongside spicy dishes.

INGREDIENTS
2 large zucchinis, halved lengthways
500 gms Greek yoghurt, beaten well
2 cloves garlic, finely ground
A handful of fresh mint leaves, washed & finely chopped
Salt & pepper to taste

METHOD
1. Heat a griddle or heavy-bottomed, ridged saucepan. Lay the zucchini slices flat and grill on both sides until a little soft and marked with griddle lines and brown spots. The charred parts give a deliciously smoky flavour to the dip. When grilled, put aside and allow to cool.
2. Combine the Greek yoghurt, garlic, salt and pepper in a bowl. Mix thoroughly and set aside.
3. Roughly chop the cooled zucchini slices in a food processor.
4. Add the processed zucchini to the yoghurt mixture, together with the mint. Stir and chill for at least 30-45 minutes.
5. Serve with fresh, chopped vegetables, bread, pitta sticks, or even with corn crackers.

NOTE
➢ As a variation, you can serve it sprinkled with fresh pomegranate seeds or chopped walnuts.

CRUNCHY SALAD
~ EUROPE ~

INGREDIENTS
½ small white cabbage (approx. 225gms)
1 small red onion
1 red pepper
3 sticks celery
50 gms wild rocket/watercress

For the Dressing
4 tbsp yogurt
2 tsp olive oil
2 tsp orange zest (grated orange rind)
1-2 tbsp orange juice
¼ tsp salt
2 tsp sesame, roasted (optional)

METHOD
1. Finely slice the cabbage and onion (use a food processor if you prefer).
2. De-seed and dice the pepper.
3. Chop celery diagonally into thin slices.
4. Mix the salad ingredients (except the wild rocket/watercress) in a bowl.
5. Stir together all the dressing ingredients (except the sesame, if being used).
6. Unless serving immediately, keep the salad and dressing in the fridge. Before serving, pour the dressing over the salad and toss to mix.
7. Garnish with wild rocket/watercress and sprinkle the sesame, if using. Serve immediately.

NOTES
➢ Instead of slicing, the cabbage can be shredded.
➢ Adjust the seasoning and the quantity of dressing to taste.

DE PUY LENTIL WARM SALAD
~ FRANCE ~

French de Puy lentils look similar to other green lentils but taste quite different and hold their shape and texture much better. This warm salad can be made with any flat green lentils but du Puy lentils give an authentic taste.

INGREDIENTS
250 gms de Puy lentils
4 stalks spring onions, sliced into fine rings
100 gms cherry tomatoes, halved
50 gms goat's cheese, crumbled
For the Dressing
6 tbsp olive/vegetable oil
2 tbsp red wine vinegar
2 tbsp fresh thyme/1 tbsp dried thyme
2 tsp Dijon mustard
4 cloves garlic, made into paste
Salt & freshly ground black pepper to taste
Olive oil for drizzling

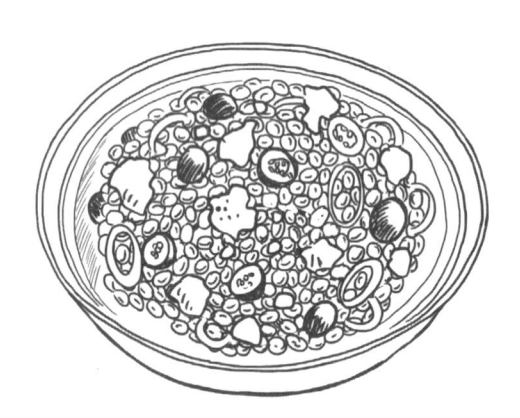

METHOD
1. Rinse the lentils thoroughly until the water runs clear. Put them into a deep saucepan with plenty of water and bring to a boil. Lower heat and simmer gently until the lentils are beginning to turn tender but still retain their bite.
2. While the lentils are cooking, prepare the dressing. Whisk together all the dressing ingredients and set aside.
3. Once the lentils have cooked, drain them and while still warm, add the dressing. Stir through gently to mix. Some of the dressing will be absorbed by the warm lentils as well.
4. Add in the spring onions and cherry tomatoes. Toss gently.
5. Crumble a little goat's cheese on the salad and drizzle some olive oil. Serve with warm bread rolls.

FENNEL & TOMATO SALAD
~ EUROPE ~

Fresh fennel adds a unique flavour to dishes, especially to salads when used raw. Baby fennel bulbs have a light aniseed taste and are best for salads while the larger bulbs with their strong anise flavour, are better for cooking. The addition of fresh fennel to this traditional combination of tomatoes, basil and pine nuts, is truly delicious.

INGREDIENTS
250 gms cherry/plum tomatoes, halved
3 tbsp pine nuts
½ small bulb fennel, halved, cored & finely sliced
A handful of fresh basil leaves, roughly torn
3 tbsp olive oil
1 tbsp red wine vinegar/lemon juice
Salt to taste
Freshly ground black pepper to taste

METHOD
1. In a small pan, dry roast the pine nuts gently for 1-2 minutes until they begin to turn golden brown.
2. Combine all the ingredients, including the pine nuts, in a salad bowl. Toss gently to mix well. Let the salad rest for at least 30 minutes to allow the flavours to develop and blend.

NOTE
➢ Sometimes the fennel bulbs have fine, dill-like leaves on top. Chop and scatter on the salad before serving to add even more freshness and nutrients.

FENNEL, CARROT & ORANGE SALAD
~ EUROPE ~

This colourful and fresh salad can be enjoyed on its own or as an accompaniment to a stew or pasta main course.

Ingredients
1 medium-sized fennel bulb, halved, cored & finely sliced
1 large juicy sweet orange
2 medium-sized carrots, peeled & julienned
1 tsp orange zest (grated orange rind)
1 tbsp sunflower seeds, lightly toasted
2 tbsp olive/any light vegetable oil
1 tbsp lemon juice
Salt & freshly ground black pepper
50 gms feta cheese (optional), for scattering

Method
1. Prepare the orange first by lightly grating the rind until you have 1 tsp zest. Grate lightly to ensure you get only the orange skin and not the white bitter pith inside. Set aside.
2. Using a sharp knife, slice off about ½ cm off the top and bottom so the orange can sit flat. With the knife, peel off the skin and pith so you are left with just the fleshy part of the orange. Using the same sharp knife, hold the orange in one hand and with the other, start slicing the orange segments close to the white dividing membrane. Slice through on both sides of each membrane, going to the core of the orange, and each orange segment will fall out. Do this over a bowl to catch all the juices along with the segments.
3. Prepare the dressing by whisking together the oil, lemon juice, salt and pepper.
4. In a large salad bowl, combine the orange segments (including the juice), fennel slices, julienned carrots and sunflower seeds. Drizzle in the dressing and toss gently to mix well.
5. Serve in salad bowl with a scattering of crumbled feta.

GREEN BEAN SALAD
~ EUROPE ~

INGREDIENTS
500 gms beans, cut length ways
½ cup hazel/nuts of choice, chopped & roasted
½ cup mayonnaise
¼ cup lemon zest and juice
1 tsp mustard paste
½ cup fresh chives/herb of choice, finely chopped
Crushed pepper to taste

METHOD
1. Bring the beans to boil in a little water. Simmer till tender but chewy (a few minutes).
2. Drain and then mix in all the other ingredients while the beans are still warm.

NOTE
➢ A clove of crushed garlic can be added for extra flavour.

GREEN LENTIL SALAD
~ GREECE ~
As the lentils for this salad are kept firm, the dish has a nutty taste.

INGREDIENTS
1 cup green lentils, soaked
1 medium-sized onion, finely chopped
2-3 tbsp lemon juice/wine vinegar
4 tbsp olive oil
Salt & pepper to taste
½ tsp sugar
½ cup fresh mint or coriander, finely chopped

METHOD
1. Boil the lentils in just enough water to soften them. Simmer to get a chewy consistency (*al dente*).
2. Drain the water. While the lentils are still warm mix in all the ingredients. Taste and add extra salt or lemon as required.
3. Serve warm or at room temperature.

NOTES
- Green chilli can be used instead of pepper.
- ½ capsicum, diced fine, can be added in step 2.

GREEN POTATO SALAD
~ IRAN/MOROCCO/TURKEY ~

This is a comforting salad with healthy herbs and tongue-tingling sweet and salty flavours.

INGREDIENTS
250 gms floury potatoes
1 cup parsley, finely chopped
1 cup dill, finely chopped
½ cup mint, finely chopped
100 gms feta cheese
6-8 tbsp olive oil
3-4 tbsp lemon juice
Salt to taste
Freshly ground black pepper to taste
1 ripe pomegranate's seeds (arils)

METHOD
1. Gently whisk together the oil, lemon juice, pepper and salt in a mixing bowl. Set aside.
2. Boil the potatoes in a large saucepan of hot water. They should be cooked through but not mushy.
3. Drain and quickly peel the potatoes while they are still hot. Use a fork to hold the hot potato in one hand and remove the peel using a knife if necessary, with the other hand. Place the peeled potatoes in a covered bowl and cut or break into bite-sized pieces.
4. Pour the oil mixture over the potatoes. Stir gently to coat. The warm potatoes will soak up the oil and flavours.
5. Sprinkle in the herbs and mix again.
6. Sprinkle the crushed feta cheese and pomegranate seeds and serve.

SALADS

PANZANELLA

~ ITALY ~

Basil and tomatoes are a heavenly pairing. You cannot go wrong with this panzanella, *a bread-based salad from Tuscany. It is also an innovative way of using stale bread. Originally a peasant dish, it has become popular as a fresh, light and healthy meal option.*

INGREDIENTS
For the Salad
3 cups chunks of stale white bread
4 large ripe tomatoes, diced
1 medium-sized red onion, halved & finely sliced
1 large cucumber, deseeded & diced
For the Dressing
6 tbsp olive oil
3 tbsp red wine vinegar/lemon juice
12-15 basil leaves, roughly torn
1 tsp garlic paste
Salt & black pepper to taste

METHOD
1. Combine all the salad ingredients in a large salad bowl and toss gently. Leave to rest for 30-40 minutes so the tomato juices infuse, soften and refresh the stale bread.
2. Prepare the dressing by whisking together all the dressing ingredients.
3. After 30-40 minutes, drizzle the dressing over the salad. Toss to mix and leave for another 10 minutes for all the flavours to mingle, then serve fresh.

NOTES
➢ If you do not have any stale bread, use crusty fresh bread which will not go soggy too quickly.
➢ You can also toast the bread to make it crispy and retain its structure in the salad.
➢ As a variation, try Fattoush, a similar Middle Eastern dish, which uses stale pitta bread. They also use more herbs (parsley, mint and coriander), instead of just basil.

POTATOES WITH SOUR CREAM
~ EUROPE ~

INGREDIENTS
500 gms waxy potatoes
½ cup chives, finely chopped
½ cup parsley, finely chopped
1 cup sour cream
1 tbsp Dijon mustard
2 tbsp olive oil
1 tbsp red wine vinegar
Salt & pepper to taste

METHOD
1. Place the potatoes in a large saucepan, cover with hot water and boil till cooked. Drain and once cool, peel and dice into 2 cm cubes. Place the cubed potatoes in a salad bowl and set aside.
2. In a small bowl, whisk together the mustard, olive oil, vinegar, salt and pepper.
3. Slowly add the sour cream to this mixture, whisking gently with a fork to fold in the cream.
4. Scatter the parsley and chives and then drizzle in the sour cream mixture onto the cubed potatoes. Mix gently until the potatoes are well coated with the herbs and dressing. Serve fresh.

NOTE
➢ This mellow and creamy side dish goes well with a spicy or more robust-flavoured main course.

QUINOA HERBY SALAD
~ MIDDLE EAST ~

This refreshing and herby salad is traditionally made with cous cous or tabbouleh. As a variation, this recipe uses quinoa, *a nutritious grain with a nutty flavour. You can also crumble some feta cheese on top.*

INGREDIENTS
For the Salad
1 cup *quinoa*, soaked for 5 mins, drained & rinsed
2 ½ cups water
1 red pepper, diced
1 yellow pepper, diced
1 medium-sized cucumber, diced
¼ cup finely sliced spring onions
4 cherry tomatoes, diced
½ cup finely chopped, parsley
½ cup finely chopped mint
¼ tsp salt
For the Dressing
6 tbsp olive oil
3 tbsp red wine vinegar/lemon juice
Salt & black pepper to taste

METHOD
1. Bring the water to boil in a medium-sized saucepan and add in the salt and quinoa. Bring back to the boil, then turn the heat to low. Cover the pan and let the quinoa cook. Check after 10 minutes. If the quinoa is clear and you can see the little threads, it is ready. Test to ensure it is soft but not mushy. Drain off any excess water and fluff up the quinoa with a fork and leave to cool.
2. In a separate bowl, combine all the remaining salad ingredients.
3. Add in the cooled quinoa and mix gently.
4. In a separate bowl, whisk together the dressing ingredients and drizzle over the salad. Toss gently to thoroughly infuse. Serve with toasted pitta chips.

SALADS

RED CABBAGE WITH NUTS
~ UKRAINE ~

This more-ish, crispy-crunchy salad has nuts and other healthy ingredients, making it high in nutritional value. A bowl of this colourful and tempting fare, along with some bread, makes for a light and delicious lunch.

INGREDIENTS
1 cup finely shredded red cabbage
½ cup grated carrot
2 stalks finely chopped celery
1 small apple, thinly sliced lengthways
4 leaves crispy lettuce (gem or web), broken into small bits
½ cup fresh pomegranate seeds
½ cup roughly chopped fresh herb of choice
½ cup mayonnaise
½ cup orange juice
1 tsp granulated mustard
¾ cup nuts and seeds of choice, roasted & crushed
¼ cup sultanas

METHOD
1. Assemble all the ingredients in a large bowl.
2. Mix well before serving, ensuring the mayo and mustard have blended nicely into the salad.

NOTE
➢ White cabbage can be used if red is unavailable.

RED MELON & FETA SALAD

~ MEDITERRANEAN ~

This salad is both a visual feast with all its contrasting colours as well as extremely flavoursome with its sweet, salty and minty flavours.

INGREDIENTS
250 gms red, seedless water melon, peeled & cubed
150 gms feta cheese, crumbled
75 gms fresh mint, finely chopped
Freshly ground black pepper to taste

METHOD
1. Use seedless melon if possible but if it is not available, then remove the seeds before cutting into bite-sized pieces.
2. In a large salad bowl, combine and gently toss the melon and mint.
3. Spread out the melon-mint on a large salad platter and sprinkle the crumbled feta over. Grind some fresh pepper over it all and serve.

NOTES
- There is no need for salt as the feta is salty enough.
- Do not mix the feta into the salad, leave it crumbled over the melon and mint otherwise the salt from the feta will draw out all the juices from the melon and make the salad soggy.
- It is best to combine the melon and mint beforehand but crumble over the feta just before serving.

SHREDDED SALAD WITH TAHINI DRESSING
~ MIDDLE EAST ~

Tahini is a great base for a salad dressing when you need creaminess without using dairy or mayonnaise. The thick, sticky sesame paste can be difficult to whisk as it seizes up at first. But with the gradual addition of hot water, it will thin and achieve a dressing consistency.

INGREDIENTS
2 cups finely shredded white cabbage
2 cups finely shredded carrots
1 cup (canned) sweet corn
1 tbsp sesame seeds, lightly roasted
For the Dressing
1 cup tahini (sesame paste)
½ cup olive/any vegetable oil
2 tbsp lemon juice
2 tsp dried mint
1 tbsp honey
Salt to taste
Freshly ground black pepper to taste
1 cup hot water

METHOD
1. In a large salad bowl, combine the shredded cabbage, carrots and corn. Set aside.
2. Prepare the dressing either in a food processor or by whisking manually. Combine all the dressing ingredients, using only half the hot water at first. Drizzle in the rest slowly as you continue whisking, to loosen the sesame paste. Monitor the consistency of the dressing. The finished dressing should be runny like light cream but not thin. Add hot water slowly to achieve that consistency. Pour the dressing over the salad and toss gently to mix.

NOTES
➢ The tahini dressing can be used with any variety of salad.
➢ You can vary the flavours by substituting other herbs for the mint.

SPROUTED BEAN SALAD
~ EUROPE ~

Packed with nutrition and carrying a sweet-sour tang, this salad is a treat for the taste buds.

INGREDIENTS
1 cup mixed sprouted beans
¼ cup bulgur wheat
4 tbsp French dressing
1 clove garlic, crushed
½ cup roughly chopped fresh parsley
Salt & pepper to taste

METHOD
1. Cook the bulgur wheat in ¾ cup water over low heat till soft (or steam it).
2. In 1-2 tbsp water, cook the beans for 1 minute.
3. While still hot, mix in all the other ingredients. Serve hot or at room temperature.

NOTE
➢ For extra colour and flavour ½ a grated carrot and crispy lettuce can be added.

TOMATO WITH PINE NUTS
~ EUROPE ~

Salads are not only healthy but make appetizing side dishes and light meals while adding colour, flavour and zest.

INGREDIENTS
3 large tomatoes (approx ½ kg)
3 tbsp olive oil
1 tbsp lime juice
3 tbsp pine kernels/almond flakes, toasted
¼ cup chopped fresh mint/coriander
Salt & crushed pepper to taste

METHOD
1. Chop the tomatoes into bite-size cubes.
2. Mix all the ingredients and serve.

NOTE
➢ For extra flavour and spice, add a clove of crushed garlic.

TOMATO SALSA

~ MEXICO ~

Salsa is the perfect accompaniment for cheesy quesadillas. The tangy, hot blend makes for an appetizing treat.

INGREDIENTS
3 large tomatoes, chopped finely
1 large red/white onion, chopped finely
2 tbsp lemon juice
1-2 green chilli, finely chopped
½ tsp sugar
Salt to taste
2 tbsp olive oil
1 cup finely chopped fresh coriander

METHOD
1. Mix all the ingredients.
2. Serve with hot quesadillas or nachos.

NOTE
➢ If preferred, peel the tomatoes before dicing. To peel: prick the tomatoes, place them in a deep bowl and cover with boiling water. In a minute or so, when the skin splits, remove from water and peel.

VIETNAMESE SALAD
~ VIETNAM ~

Vietnamese salads have a range of strong flavours and are most satisfying. The spicy, sweet, sour and salty salads can be eaten as a main or side dish. The usual dash of fish sauce has been omitted in this vegetarian recipe.

INGREDIENTS
For the Salad
2 medium-sized carrots, peeled & julienned
50 gms bean sprouts
50 gms white cabbage, shredded into fine strips
A handful of coriander leaves, roughly chopped
50 gms peanuts, roasted & roughly crushed
2 stalks spring onions, cut diagonally into fine rings
For the Dressing
3 tbsp rice vinegar/lime juice
1 tsp caster sugar
2 tbsp light soy sauce/orange juice
2 red chillies, cut diagonally into fine rings
Salt to taste

METHOD
1. Whisk together all the dressing ingredients, ensuring the sugar dissolves completely. Set aside.
2. In a large salad bowl, combine all the salad ingredients, keeping aside 2 tbsp crushed peanuts and 1 tbsp coriander leaves for garnishing.
3. Dress the salad only when you are ready to eat to ensure the ingredients remain crisp and crunchy. When ready, drizzle the dressing over the salad and toss gently. Serve with a sprinkling of the reserved peanuts and coriander.

NOTE
➢ As a variation, you can add browned tofu pieces to the salad and enjoy it as main dish.

ZUCCHINI SALAD
~ EUROPE ~

INGREDIENTS
2 large zucchinis, chopped diagonally into 2 mm thick pieces
2 tbsp olive oil
3 tbsp lemon juice
1 clove garlic, finely chopped
1 tbsp fresh herb of choice
10-12 almonds (optional), chopped & roasted
Salt & pepper to taste

METHOD
Heat oil in a large pan and toss in all ingredients. Cook for 1-2 minutes (the zucchini to be *al dente*). Serve hot.

NOTE
➢ This salad can be made with capsicum instead of zucchini.

VINAIGRETTE
~ FRANCE ~

INGREDIENTS
¼ cup wine/cider vinegar
¼ cup olive oil
½ tbsp honey/sugar
Salt & pepper to taste

METHOD
Place all the ingredients in a bottle, close the lid tight and shake till well blended. It can be kept for a long time. You can make it more sour, according to taste.

Harissa Paste

~ MEDITERRANAN/NORTH AFRICA ~

Harissa paste is found in some Middle Eastern and Northern African cuisines. It is a fiery hot, red-orange paste made with red chilli peppers and spices. It can be made in a small quantity for a meal or stored in jars to last a week in the fridge.

INGREDIENTS
10-12 dry hot red chillies
1 tbsp ground coriander seeds
1 tbsp ground cumin seeds
4-6 fresh cloves garlic, peeled
Olive oil (optional)
Salt to taste

METHOD
1. Soften the chillies by soaking them in hot water for an hour. Remove and retain the water.
2. Remove the chilli stalks and roughly chop the chillies. Add in the garlic cloves, ground coriander seeds, ground cumin seeds and salt.
3. Grind the mixture in a mortar and pestle or food processor, until a loose consistency has been achieved. Add spoonfuls of the retained water if the mixture is too dry and needs to be loosened.
4. Use in your recipe straight away. To preserve the paste, store it in an airtight jar with a layer of olive oil on top to prevent it from drying out.

NOTES
➢ Harissa paste can be used in a range of recipes and is particularly good for flavouring cous cous.
➢ It can also be used as a relish to add a touch of heat to otherwise bland dishes.

HONEY VINAIGRETTE
~ FRANCE ~

INGREDIENTS
½ cup balsamic vinegar
¼ cup olive oil
2 tbsp honey
1 tbsp granulated mustard
Salt & pepper to taste

METHOD
Put all the ingredients into a bottle, close the lid tight and shake till well blended. The vinaigrette can be made more sweet or sour according to taste. Store and use as required.

LEMON MAYONNAISE
~ EUROPE ~

INGREDIENTS
½ cup thick mayo
Zest & juice of ½ lemon
1 tbsp granulated mustard
Dry herb of choice

METHOD
Place all ingredients in a bottle, close the lid tight and shake till well blended. This can be stored in the fridge for a week or so.

Desserts & Afters

APPLE CRUMBLE
~ UK ~

INGREDIENTS
For the Crumble
60 gms plain flour
30 gms oats
80 gms unsalted butter & to grease the dish
40 gms caster sugar

For the filling
500 gms cooking apples or a tart variety (e.g. Granny Smith)
40 gms demerara sugar
Zest of 1 lemon
1 tbsp lemon juice
1 tbsp water
¼ tsp ground cinnamon
3 cloves

METHOD
1. Sift the flour in a bowl. Cut the butter into cubes and add to the flour. Rub with your fingertips, adding in the oats, until the mixture resembles breadcrumbs. Add the caster sugar and mix. Leave in the fridge until you have prepared the apples.
2. Core, peel (only if using cooking apples) and slice the apples. Add the demerara sugar, cinnamon, cloves, lemon zest, juice and water and mix. Spoon the mixture into a shallow, greased ovenproof dish and cover with the crumble mix.
3. Preheat the oven to 180°C and bake for 40-45 minutes or till the crumble turns golden brown and the fruit is hot and bubbling. Serve with custard, cream or ice cream.

NOTES
➢ Crumbles can be made using a variety of fruits such as rhubarb, gooseberries or a mix of fruits.
➢ The quantity of sugar should be adjusted according to the tartness of the fruit.

APPLE & PLUM CAKE
~ EUROPE ~

INGREDIENTS
300 gms cooking apples, peeled, cored & sliced
200 gms plums, destoned & quartered
65-75 gms demerara sugar
125 gms caster sugar
125 gms butter
2 eggs, lightly beaten
100 gms self-raising flour, sifted
50 gms ground almond
½ tsp vanilla essence
1 tsp mixed spice
Finely grated rind of 1 lemon

METHOD
1. Layer a greased, ovenproof dish with the apple slices and sprinkle half the demerara sugar, half the mixed spice and some of the lemon rind. Repeat the above with a layer of plums.
2. Beat the butter and caster sugar until light and fluffy. Lightly beat the eggs and add a little at a time to the butter and sugar mixture, adding a little flour to the last amount to avoid curdling. Add the rest of the flour, ground almond and vanilla essence and mix well.
3. Spread the cake mixture evenly over the fruit. Preheat oven to 180°C and bake for 35-40 minutes until golden brown and springy to the touch. Test with a cocktail stick/ tooth pick/skewer – when inserted in the centre of the cake, it should come out clean.
4. Serve hot as a dessert with cream/ice cream/custard; or on its own at tea time.

NOTES
➢ Replace plums with apples; and mixed spice with cinnamon; to make Eve's Pudding. The apples are concealed under the sponge cake hence the biblical reference to Eve and the tree of knowledge.
➢ Use seasonal fruits such as gooseberries, rhubarb or a mix of fruits.

CAKE PUDDING WITH ORANGE
~ BRAZIL ~

Brazil has an exciting mix of African and Portuguese culinary traditions. The abundance of fruits and vegetables there also make for interesting vegetarian options. This recipe is an improvisation on their many fruit-based puddings.

INGREDIENTS
For the Orange-in-Syrup
2 oranges, sliced into thin rounds
¾ cup sugar
1-2 cinnamon sticks
4-6 peppercorns
¼ cup dark rum
For the Pudding
2 cups broken pieces of stale cake
2 cups single cream
½ cup almonds/pistachio, roughly chopped & toasted
1 orange rind
½ cup grated dark chocolate

METHOD
Orange-in-Syrup
1. In a large pan, melt the sugar (adding a spoon or two of water), over low heat. Once it starts bubbling, add the orange slices, cinnamon and peppers. Ladle the sugar syrup onto the oranges and leave to stew for 10 minutes or till most of the liquid has dried out.
2. When cool, mix in the rum. This can be stored in a jar for months.

Pudding
1. Mix the cake pieces, cream, nuts and orange rind in a glass serving bowl. Sprinkle the grated chocolate and leave in a cool place for a few hours.
2. Place a slice of orange on a small plate and arrange a generous scoop of pudding on top to serve.

NOTE
➢ The pudding can be made with stale brioche or chocolate biscuits and fruits like kiwi can be used.

DRY FRUITS & NUTS COMPOTE
~ MIDDLE EAST ~

Compotes are among the easiest and most elegant desserts and can be varied depending on the dried fruits and nuts used. Most cultures have a version of this dessert. The fruits and nuts used in this recipe are reflective of Middle Eastern desserts.

INGREDIENTS
100 gms dried figs, cut into bite-sized pieces
100 gms dried pitted apricots, cut into bite-sized pieces
50 gms dried dates, cut into bite-sized pieces
50 gms cashew nuts, chopped
50 gms almonds, chopped
50 gms pistachio kernels, chopped
1 litre orange juice
½ tsp saffron strands
To serve: cream/crème fraiche/ice-cream

METHOD
1. Roughly break the nuts with gentle pulsing in a food processor or mortar and pestle. You should end with broken nuts rather than powder.
2. In a deep and heavy-bottomed saucepan, combine the fruits and nuts. Pour in the orange juice and stir to ensure all the fruits are covered. Place on low heat to warm up gently.
3. Once warm, stir in the saffron and simmer gently until all the fruit has plumped up, softened and is swimming in a thickened orange liquid. This could take up to 30-45 minutes.
4. Serve chilled in summer and warmed up in winter, along with fresh cream.

NOTES
➢ There is no need for any sugar as the dried fruits bring in plenty of sweetness.
➢ Use different dried fruits and nuts to create variety.
➢ For a more sophisticated taste, add 4 tbsp Amaretto di Saronno liqueur with the orange juice.

GREEK STYLE SEMOLINA CAKE
~ GREECE ~

INGREDIENTS
2 cups semolina
1 cup roughly chopped mixed nuts
 (almonds, pistachio, hazelnuts, walnuts)
2 cups sugar
3 eggs
1 cup oil
2 tbsp thick sour yoghurt
1 tsp baking powder
Rind of 1 lime, finely grated

For the Topping
Juice of 1 lime
4 tbsp sugar
¼ cup mixed nuts, roughly chopped

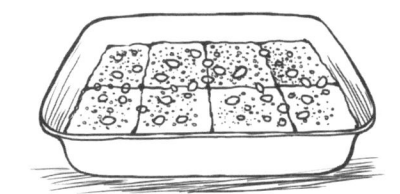

METHOD
1. In a large bowl, whisk together the sugar, oil and eggs till creamy and fluffy.
2. Add the yoghurt, semolina and baking powder and whisk till blended into a smooth paste.
3. Using a wooden spoon, fold in the nuts and lime rind.
4. Pour the batter into a well greased, square baking tray. Bake at 200°C for 30 minutes. Check the cake has set and is golden on top (if required, bake for another 5-10 minutes).

Topping
1. In a saucepan, heat the lime juice and sugar. As soon as it boils, add the nuts. Simmer for a minute and then take off the heat and spread evenly on top of the cake.
2. When the cake has cooled, cut into squares to serve.

NOTE
➢ This cake goes very well with a medley of diced fruits on the side.

IRISH COFFEE CAKE
~ EUROPE ~

If you use non-Irish whisky to make this cake, please refer to it as Coffee & Whisky Cake.

INGREDIENTS
For the Cake
150 gms self-raising flour, sifted
150 gms butter
150 gms castor sugar
3 large eggs, lightly beaten

For the Irish Coffee
355 ml strong, freshly brewed coffee
2 tbsp brown sugar
6 tbsp Irish whisky

To Decorate
250 ml whipping cream (36%-40% fat), lightly whipped
2 tbsp flaked almonds, toasted

METHOD
1. Preheat the oven to 180°C.
2. Beat the butter and sugar until light, creamy and fluffy.
3. Gradually beat in the eggs, adding a tablespoon of flour with the last amount.
4. Fold in the rest of the flour gently.
5. Line the base of a greased 20 cm cake tin with greased greaseproof paper and pour in the cake batter. Bake for 40-45 minutes or till golden brown. A skewer, or cocktail stick inserted comes out clean. Leave in tin.
6. Add the sugar to the coffee and stir until completely dissolved. Blend in the whisky.
7. Transfer the cake onto a serving plate and pierce all over with Check if a skewer or a cocktail stick.
8. Pour a small amount of coffee over the cake. Once absorbed, pour some more. Continue this process until all the coffee is used up. Rest the cake for 4-5 hours.
9. Spread the cream over the cake and sprinkle with toasted almonds to serve.

PANJIREE

~ INDIA ~

The variety of Indian sweets is endless – made with fruits, vegetables, cereals, pulses and milk and milk products. The beauty of this recipe is that it takes just 20 minutes to make something people will love.

INGREDIENTS
3 cups gram flour (approx 300 gms)
200 gms (unsalted) butter or ghee
450 gms (1 tin) condensed milk (sweet)
8 pods cardamom, finely crushed
20 almonds, finely chopped

METHOD
1. Melt all but 1 teaspoon of the butter in a large, heavy-bottomed pan and stir in the gram flour. Cook on gentle heat till the flour has browned.
2. In another pan (use a heavy pan so the milk doesn't catch at the bottom), bring the condensed milk to a boil.
3. Add in the cardamom and pour the boiling liquid into the still hot gram flour. Mix well.
4. Grease a 10 inch shallow dish with a teaspoon of butter and then spread the mixture evenly.
5. Sprinkle the almonds and pat them down gently. Allow to cool.
6. Once cool, cut into desired size pieces. This sweet will keep for at least a week and longer in the fridge. It can be frozen as well.

NOTE
➢ To give the sweet a nuttier taste, use double the amount of almonds and add them while the gram flour is being roasted.

PEARS WITH SAFFRON & HONEY
~ MIDDLE EAST ~

This dish of tender poached pears in a golden saffron syrup, is a refreshing way to end a meal. It can be served warm or cold, depending on the weather.

INGREDIENTS
4 pears, firm but not ripe
7-8 tbsp clear honey or to taste
¼ tsp saffron strands
4 cm cinnamon stick
4 cups freshly boiled water
2 tbsp flaked almonds, lightly toasted
To serve: ice cream/cream

METHOD
1. Put the water into a medium-sized pan. Add the cinnamon stick, honey and saffron and bring to a boil. Leave on low heat to simmer while you prepare the pears.
2. Wash and peel the pears, leaving the stalks intact. Put the pears into the simmering pan as soon as you peel each one, to avoid them becoming discoloured. Turn up the heat to medium and simmer for about 30-40 minutes until the pears are just tender. Remove with a slotted spoon and set aside.
3. Increase the heat and simmer the remaining liquid until it has reduced to a light syrup.
4. When ready to eat, place a pear in each dessert bowl and pour a couple of spoonfuls of syrup over it. Sprinkle with some flaked almonds and serve with ice cream or cream.

PINEAPPLE UPSIDE DOWN CAKE
~ UK ~

INGREDIENTS
430 gms canned sliced pineapple in own or fruit juice
100 gms sugar
100 gms butter
100 gms self-raising flour, sifted
2 tbsp golden syrup
5-6 hulled strawberries/glacé cherries
50 gms desiccated coconut (optional)
2 eggs, lightly beaten

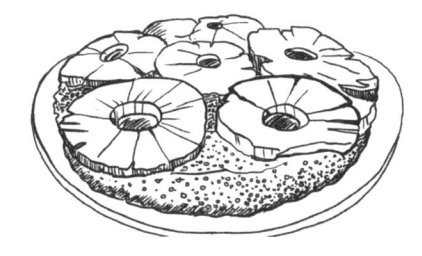

METHOD
1. Grease a 20 cm fixed base cake tin and line the base with greased greaseproof paper.
2. Spread the golden syrup on the base.
3. Drain and arrange the pineapple slices on the syrup. Place a strawberry or glacé cherry in the centre of each pineapple slice.
4. Preheat oven to 180°C.
5. Cream the butter and sugar until light and fluffy.
6. Beat in the eggs gradually, adding 1-2 tablespoons flour with the last amount to avoid curdling.
7. Mix in the coconut (if using).
8. Carefully fold in the flour and pour the mixture into the cake tin. Bake for 35-45 minutes or until a skewer/cocktail stick inserted in the centre comes out clean. Serve warm or at room temperature, on its own or with cream or custard.

NOTE
➢ Fresh or tinned apricot halves can be used instead of pineapple. On the base of the cake tin, place the cut sides of the apricot facing down with a glacé cherry in the centre of the fruit.

SUMMER PUDDING
~ UK ~

Despite the erratic weather in the UK, spring and summer days can be absolutely glorious. During summer season there is a profusion of soft fruits and berries throughout the land, growing in gardens, wastelands, roadside bushes and allotments. There is a long standing tradition of individuals and families going on walks, collecting the berries and turning them into jam, crumbles, tarts and other enticing fares such as Summer Pudding.

INGREDIENTS
3 cups mixed berries
 (strawberry, raspberry, blueberry, blackberry, gooseberry etc.)
1 cup sugar (more if the fruits are very tart)
A few sprigs fresh mint
8-10 slices superior white bread, all sides trimmed
1½ cups single cream

METHOD
1. Mix the fruits and sugar and put aside for an hour or so.
2. Completely line the base and sides of a 1 litre, round glass bowl, with the bread slices (keeping enough for the top).
3. Pour the fruit mix into the lined bowl and top with bread, ensuring there are no gaps.
4. Weigh the top down with a plate and gently press the pudding (the bread will soak up the fruit juices and change colour). Leave the pudding in a cool place overnight.
5. To serve: carefully loosen the pudding from all sides, and place a large serving plate on top of the bowl and turn upside down. The pudding will retain the shape of the bowl. Decorate with mint. Slice and serve with cream.

NOTES
➢ The pudding can also be made with stale dry cake.
➢ Instead of cream, serve with ice-cream.

TRIFLE
~ UK ~

INGREDIENTS
Small flan case or sponge cake
300 gms canned fruit cocktail in fruit juice
OR seasonal fresh fruits of your choice.
20 ml fruit juice, if using fresh fruit, for additional moisture
2 tbsp sherry (optional)
1 packet vegetarian jelly, in a flavour of your choice
568 ml milk
2 tbsp custard powder
1-2 tbsp sugar
2 tsp vanilla extract
250 ml whipping cream
2 tbsp almonds (optional), toasted
2 strawberries

METHOD
1. Line a wide-bottomed, deep glass bowl with the flan case. Trim the case if necessary to fit the bowl. If using sponge cake, it can be sliced to line the base of the bowl. Pierce all over with a fork and pour the sherry evenly.
2. Drain the canned fruit. Retain the juice to add later if required. Spread the canned / fresh fruit on the base. Pour additional juice (if required) so the base is moist but not soaked.
3. Make the jelly as per the instructions on the packet and cool.
4. Gently pour the jelly over the layer of fruit and leave in the fridge until set.
5. In the meantime, prepare the custard using the method below or instructions on the packet. In a bowl mix the custard powder and sugar with a little milk, taken from the 568 ml, into a smooth paste. Heat the remaining milk to nearly boiling. Add the milk to the custard paste, stir well ensuring there are no lumps. Transfer the custard mix to the saucepan and return to gentle heat. Add the vanilla extract and bring to boil on low to medium heat stirring continuously. Let it cool.

6. When the jelly is set take the trifle out of the fridge and gently and evenly pour the custard on the layer of jelly. Return to the fridge to set the custard.
7. Lightly whip the cream and spread it evenly over the custard when it is set. Sprinkle with toasted almonds and decorate with strawberries or as your imagination and creativity will let you.

NOTES
- One or two varieties of seasonal fruits or a cocktail of seasonal fruits can be used ensuring the fruits and trifle base are moist.
- You can substitute sherry with a liqueur such as Cointreau or Amaretto.

SELECT GLOSSARY

Allotment: Small plot of land in a city or town, owned by the local government but leased out to individuals to grow produce (for home consumption).
Aubergine: Vegetable also referred to as eggplant, brinjal, baigan.
Black chick peas/kala chana: chick peas, smaller than the cream colour variety. It has dark brown skin.
Bulgur wheat/Couscous: This is also known as bulghur/bulgar or cracked wheat.
Capsicum: This vegetable, also known as pepper or shimla mirch comes in a variety of colours including, green, red and orange.
Al dente: Style of cooking pasta and vegetables which preserves a slight bite to the food, maintaining food structure and taste.
Extra Virgin Olive Oil: Usually the first extraction from the olive fruits. This is the most flavoursome type of Olive Oil and ideal for salad dressings. It is not suitable for cooking or frying as the high heat destroys the flavours.
Feta cheese: Greek in origin, Feta is a salty and crumbly cheese usually made from the milk of sheep or goats. It is widely used in Mediterranean cooking and often crumbled over salads and dishes.
Galangal: Far Eastern root spice similar to fresh ginger. Fresh ginger can be used as a substitute if galangal is not available.
Green Lentils: These are a variety of small, flat, olive-green lentils often also referred to as Puy lentils. The very small type keeps its structure better and has a superior flavour to the slightly bigger types which become mushy quite quickly during the cooking process. These lentils cook quickly and therefore need to be watched to prevent them over cooking. They are good in salad dishes as well as stews.
Halloumi cheese: A semi hard salty cheese from Cyprus with a high melting point which is therefore quite easy to grill or fry and maintains its structure very well. It is generally made with a mix of goat, cow and sheep milk.
Mezze: Greek dishes of bites and nibbles served as snacks.
Mixed peel: This is a mixture of citrusy fruit rinds – usually orange and lemon. The fruit peel is cooked in sugar syrup to preserve it i.e. candied and then finely chopped and used in sweets, cakes to provide sweetness and flavour.

Mogo/Cassava: Root vegetable referred to as mogo in Africa and cassava in the USA.
Pesto: This generally refers to the Italian red and green pastes made using basil, pine nuts, olive oil, a hard cheese such as pecorino and garlic. Red pesto includes sun dried tomatoes.
Pitta: Flat bread extensively consumed in the Mediterranean, Middle East and North Africa.
Self Raising Flour: Is flour which has a raising agent (such as sodium bicarbonate) and salt already added so that the dough rises during the baking process and makes for a lighter result.
Sopa: Sopa means soup in Spanish but also refers to corn bread in Paraguay.
Sour cream: This is semi-fermented cream which has a slight tartness to it. It can be substituted by mixing thick yoghurt and cream.
Tbsp: Measurement indicating Table spoon.
Tsp: Measurement indicating Tea spoon.
Tahini: Middle Eastern sesame seed paste in oil, usually used in making hummus and often thinned out to use as dressing for salads.
Tapas: Dishes of bites and nibbles served in Spanish bars to enjoy with the drinks.
White Radish: Long white carrot like root vegetable, also known as mooli. It has a sharp hot taste and adds pungency to a dish.
Zucchini: Green, cucumber like vegetable, also referred to as courgette in some countries.

ALPHABETICAL INDEX OF DISHES

Almond Croissants *France* 21
Apple & Celery Salad *USA* 145
Apple & Plum Cake *Europe* 174
Apple Crumble *UK* 173
Apple Sauce *Germany* 122
Aubergine Parmigiana *Italy* ....
 74
Aubergine with Mozzarella *Italy* 123
Aubergine with Nuts 60
Avocado & Orange Salad *Mediterranean* 146
Avocado Bruschetta *Italy* 22
Babaganoush 61
Beetroot Salad with Dill *Europe* 147
Bori-Bori *Paraguay* 47
Bread Gnocchi *UK/Italian* 100
Broad Beans Salad 62
Broccoli & Blue Cheese Soup *Europe* 48
Broccoli with Nuts *Europe* 124
Broccoli with Orange & Almonds *Europe* .. 125
Bulgur Wheat with Sunflower Seeds *Greece,*
 Turkey, Middle East 76
Butter Beans in Pizzaiola Sauce *Italy* 77
Cake Pudding with Orange *Brazil* 175
Cannelloni *Italy* 78
Carrot with Lemon *Cuba* 148
Carrot with Peanuts *Mediterranean* 148
Cauliflower with Potatoes *Greece* 126
Charred Capsicum 63

Cheese on Toast *Europe* 35
Chickpea & Vegetable Catalan
 Soup *Spain* 49
Chickpeas & Aubergine *Lebanon* 80
Chickpeas with Mogo *E. Africa* 81
Chickpeas with Spinach Tapa 64
Chilli con Queso *Mexico* 82
Chocolate-Marzipan Tart *Europe* 36
Classic Greek Salad *Greece* 149
Corn in Buttermilk *Kenya* 127
Corn Khichdi *Kenya* 128
Corn-on-Cob Sabzi *Kenya* 83
Crêpes with Savoury Filling *France* 24
Crunchy Salad *Europe* 151
Dairy Heaven *UK/USA* 84
Date & Nut Roll *Europe* 37
De Puy Lentil Warm Salad *France* 152
Dolmas, *Greece* 65
Dry Fruits & Nuts Compote
 Middle East 176
English Breakfast *UK* 23
Feijoada Bean Stew *Brazil* 85
Fennel & Tomato Salad *Europe* 153
Fennel, Carrot & Orange Salad
 Mediterranean 154
Garlic & Paprika Soup *Spain* 50
Gazpacho *Spain* 51
Greek Style Semolina Cake *Greece* 177

Green Bean Salad *Europe*	155
Green Curry *Thailand*	87
Green Lentil Salad *Greece*	156
Green Potato Salad *Iran/Morocco/Turkey*	157
Griddle Cakes *UK*	38
Guacamole *Mexico*	129
Haggis *Scotland*	88
Harissa Paste *Mediterranean/N. Africa*	170
Honey Vinaigrette *France*	171
Hummus	67
Irish Coffee Cake *Europe*	178
Kafta Bil Tahini *Lebanon*	91
Kidney Beans & Spinach *Kenya*	93
Lablabi *Tunisia*	94
Lasagne with Aubergine *Argentina*	95
Latke *Germany/ Israel*	39
Leek with Potatoes *Germany*	52
Maharagwe ya Nazi *Kenya*	96
Marinated Olives	68
Lemon Mayonnaise *Europe*	171
Meal-in-a-Bowl *Sudan*	98
Mogo (*Cassava*) with Coconut Milk *Kenya*	40
Mushroom & Parsley Open Lasagne *Italy*	100
Mushrooms in Cream *Azerbaijan*	130
Oat Scones *UK*	41
Oatmeal Porridge *UK*	26
Okra *Middle East*	131
Onion Flan *UK*	101
Onion Soup *France*	53
Oven-Dried Tomatoes	69
Panjeeri *India*	179
Panzanella *Italy*	158
Pasta with Aubergine *Italy*	103
Patatas Bravas	70
Pears with Saffron & Honey *Middle East*	180
Peasant Soup *Italy*	55
Penne with Mozzarella *Italy*	104
Pineapple Relish *India*	132
Pineapple Upside Down Cake *UK*	181
Potato Mash *UK*	133
Potato Salad	71
Potato Skins *Mexico*	134
Potatoes with Sesame Seeds & Olives *Mediterranean*	135
Potatoes with Sour Cream & Herbs *Europe*	159
Pumpkin with Yoghurt *Afghanistan*	136
Quesadilla *Mexico*	27
Quinoa Herby Salad *Middle East*	160
Red Cabbage with Nuts *Ukraine*	161
Red Curry *Thailand*	105
Red Melon & Feta Salad *Mediterranean*	162
Ribbon Pasta with Peppers & Olives *Italy*	107
Roast Potatoes *UK*	137
Roast Pumpkin with Seeds *Europe*	138
Roasted Vegetable Slice *Mediterranean*	108
Rösti *Switzerland/Germany*	29
Savoury Muffins *Europe*	32

Scrambled Eggs with Fenugreek *Kenya*.. 30	Summer Pudding *UK* 182
Shakshuka *Mediterranean* 31	Toast with Spinach *USA* 32
Shepherd's Pie *UK* 109	Tofu, Vegetables & Cashew Stir-fry
Shredded Salad with Tahini Dressing	*China* 115
Middle East 163	Tomato Salsa *Mexico* 166
Sliced Potatoes with Cream *Latvia* 139	Tomatoes with Pine Nuts
Sopa de Ajo Blanco *Spain* 56	*Mediterranean* 165
Sopa Paraguay *Paraguay* 110	Trifle *UK* 183
Soup au Pistou *France* 57	Vegetables Roast *Greece* 116
Spicy Aubergine *Portugal* 140	Vegetarian Cacciatore *Italy* 117
Spinach Drops *UK*....................................... 43	Vegetarian Frittata *Italy* 33
Spinach with Yoghurt *Iran* 141	Vegetarian Medley *Mediterranean* 143
Spinach Quiche *France* 112	Vegetarian Salade Nicoise *France* 119
Spinach with Coconut Milk &	Vietnamese Salad *Vietnam* 167
Peanuts *Africa* 111	Vinaigrette *France* 169
Sprouted Bean Salad *Europe* 164	Welsh Rarebit *UK* 44
Stuffed Capsicum *Europe* 141	Zucchini Dip *Mediterranean* 150
Stuffed Zucchini *Europe* 114	Zucchini Salad *Europe* 168